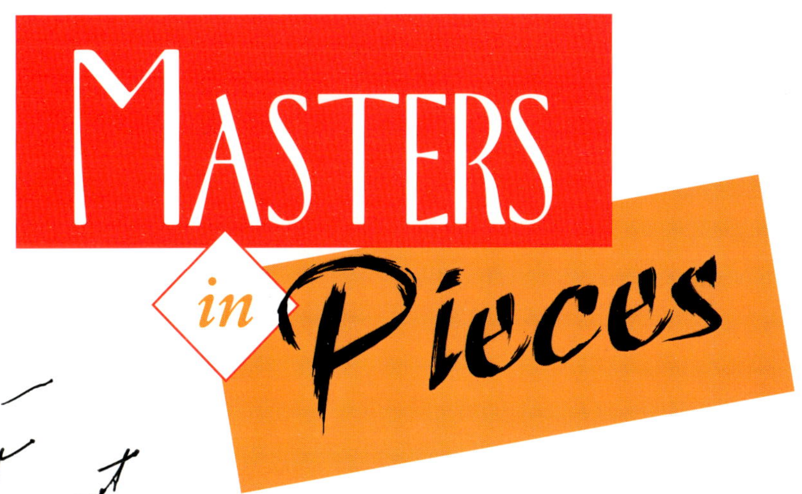

The Art of Russell Connor

To Anne — thanks for your understanding & support
Best wishes
Russell Connor
3/25/2010

By Russell Connor
Foreword by Arthur C. Danto

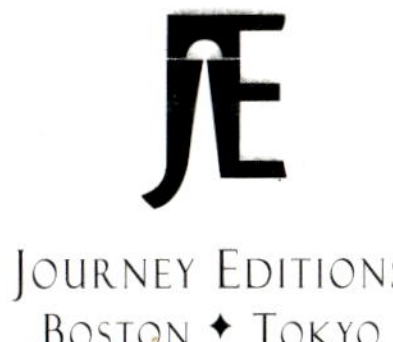

JOURNEY EDITIONS
BOSTON ✦ TOKYO

First published in 1997 by Journey Editions, an imprint of Charles E. Tuttle Co., Inc., of Rutland, Vermont, and Tokyo, Japan, with editorial offices at 153 Milk Street, Boston, Massachusetts 02109.

Library of Congress Cataloging-in-Publication Data

Connor, Russell, 1929–
Masters in pieces : the art of Russell Connor / foreword by Arthur C. Danto.
p. cm.
ISBN 1-885203-28-4
1. Connor, Russell, 1929– —Themes, motives. 2. Appropriation (Art). I. Title.
ND237.C6775A4 1997
759.13—dc20 96–28289
CIP

First edition
10 9 8 7 6 5 4 3 2 1
06 05 04 03 02 01 00 99 98 97

Design by Ralph Moxcey
Cover design by Fran Kay

Printed in Singapore

For Danny and Amy

Contents

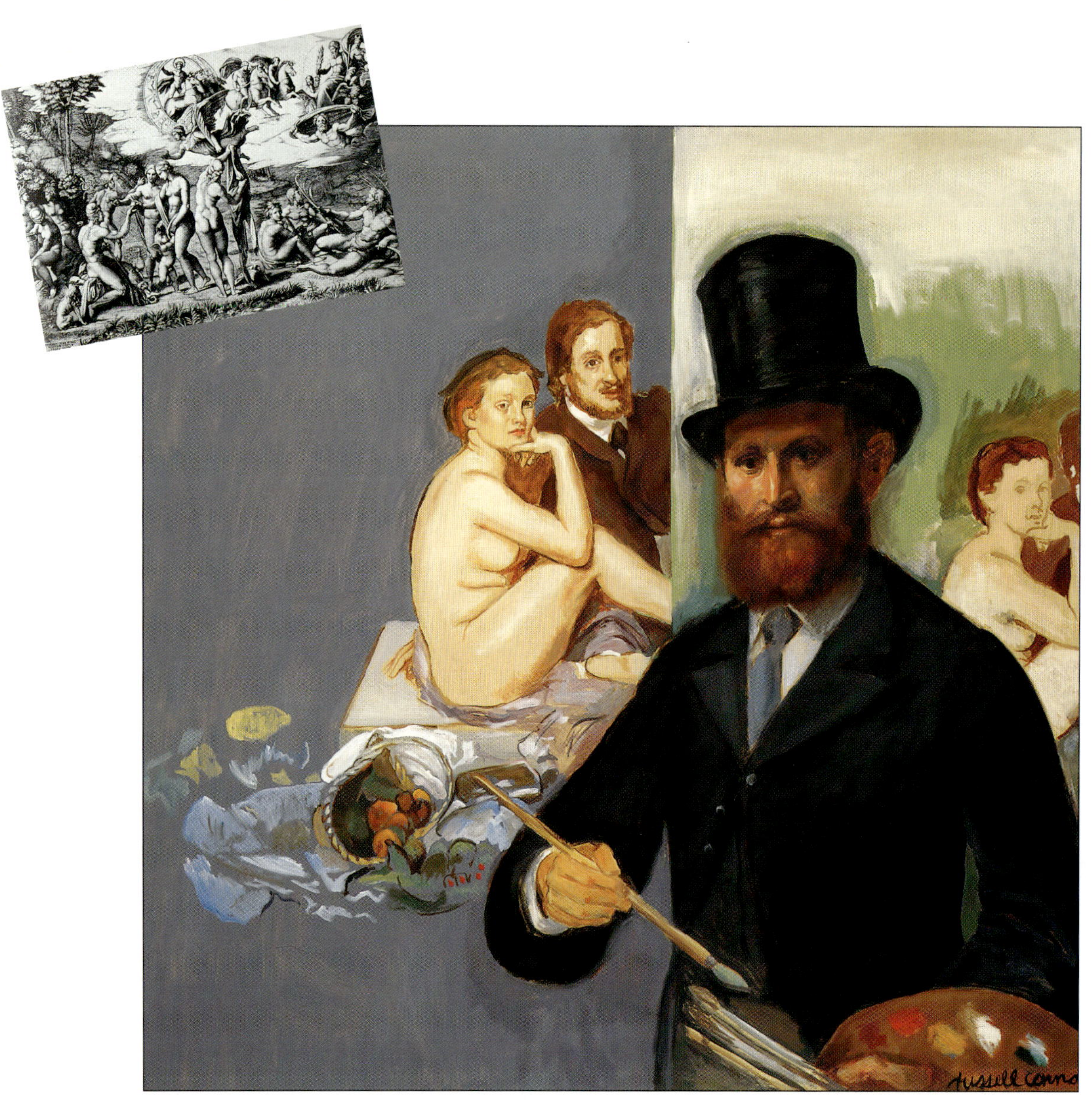

Connor and Civilized Comedy

by Arthur C. Danto

The New York Times Book Review had the happy inspiration, not long ago, of commissioning a painting from Russell Connor (left) to go with an essay on Manet. It is an expression of the Postmodern temper that an artist of his distinction felt no stigma whatever in providing a graphic image for the popular press, and Connor rose to the occasion with his characteristic deftness and wit. Manet in any case is one of his particular heroes, inasmuch as, like Connor himself, he appropriated the paintings of his heroes—Velasquez, Le Nain, Watteau, Giorgione—to his own artistic ends. In the *Times* picture, Connor shows Manet at his easel painting *Le Déjeuner sur l'herbe*, the work that was too outrageous—and too baffling—to admit to the Salon of 1863 and too good to reject out of hand. An entirely new kind of exhibition, the *Salon des Refusés*, was organized to give the public a chance to "judge for itself," as the emperor phrased it. In Connor's image, Manet is shown in the act of painting, wearing top hat and frock coat, looking away for a moment from his model and his canvas to cast a dandy's eye on us: Manet has been distracted from the task of putting into paint the famous left-hand couple—she nude, he as buttoned up as Manet himself. Probably nobody painting today could more masterfully feign Manet's way with a brush. One feels the canvas looks very much the way, in an early stage, Manet's early masterpiece looked—confident, sketchy, true.

Did Manet, in fact, pose his models as we see them depicted on the canvas, so that the four figures gathered regularly, two nude women and two heavily clothed men, day after day, as the master executed his composition, wearing top hat and frock coat? Or is Connor being maliciously literal? I am not sure we know what the studio arrangement was in those months, but we do know—Manet's contemporaries knew—that the arrangement of figures on the canvas corresponds to the arrangement of figures in a famous engraving done by the sixteenth-century master Marcantonio Raimondi after a lost drawing by Raphael. A typical Connor touch would have been to show the engraving itself, pinned to Manet's canvas, exactly in the way in which Connor pins postcards and other color reproductions to his. Had he done that, he would have made the analogy between Manet and himself explicit. As it is, the analogy extends only this far: Connor and Manet visually allude to previous works. But unless one knew, independently, about Raimondi's work, one would never have been able to tell that such an allusion was being made. Manet's inner circle might have seen in the deployment of his figures the array of mythological figures in which Raimondi's engraving partially consists, but Raimondi's work is not something most of us—Connor's contemporaries—carry in our heads.

As it happens, the title of Raimondi's print is *The Judgment of Paris* (Manet only used part of the engraving for his composition). And his friends might, if as clever as Manet, have taken the title as an anticipatory pun—being exiled to the *Salon des Refusés* was to be the judgment of Paris (France). A joke achieved through internal reference by one work of art to another is precisely in the Connor spirit. But Connor's jokes would have a different structure, in that their references are not hidden.

The Judgment of Paris shows, to its right, the figures

Manet appropriated and, in the center, the shepherd, Paris, judging which of the three goddesses merits the prize apple because of her beauty. If Connor were to paint *The Judgment of Paris*, this is how it would look: he would have Paris and the three nude goddesses just as Raimondi depicted them. And then, on the right, he would simulate—to perfection—Manet's picnicking companions, the overdressed men yammering about whatever, the undressed women silent and superior. He would conjoin, in effect, two works with an affinity waiting to be underscored. It would be chic to title the new work *Salon des Refusés!*

Alas, Raimondi's engraving is known to too few of us today to be usable for purposes of visual puns. This confines Connor's resources to art history's all-time hits, the paintings every graduate of Art History 101 knows by heart—*Olympia*, *Las Meninas*, *Les Demoiselles d'Avignon*, *Liberty Leading the People*, and many others. For viewers possessed of this degree of visual literacy (pretty much everyone literate at all), the jokes are instantaneously grasped, and the mind explodes in silent complicit laughter. We are not as clever as Manet's contemporaries, but when someone can use art as a means to engage our wit, we know at least that we are operating at the highest level of civilization allowed us. There is today a great deal of strenuous comedy, and even in very high circles, sarcasm takes itself for wit. But Connor connects us to the highest humanist tradition in the form of intellectual entertainment. So he is one with Manet on two levels. He has the visual mastery of the master. And he has the intellectual subtlety that realizes itself in jokes of the kind we find in *Déjeuner sur l'herbe*. Well, almost of that kind. The problem does not lie with the artist but with his audience: we simply lack the class and mental polish of Manet's chums. But Connor takes us at the best of which we are capable and gives us at least the semblance of what it must have been like to know what *Déjeuner sur l'herbe* was all about. That's what I call civilization! That's what I call *art!*

With Appreciation . . .

First, those whose spirits remain with me: Roy and Kathleen Connor, Tom Winfisky, Arthur Hoener, Pierre Guillery, Virginia Murphy, Winifred (Winkie) Booth, Patrick Gavin, Otis Philbrick, Josef Albers, William Seitz.

Among the precious living, Toshiko Okada Connor stands out, first, for being herself, for sharing my life for many years with patience, understanding, and humor, and for doing the lion's share of raising and nurturing our two courageous and inspiring children through some very difficult times. My brothers, Roy and Robert, and our late-arriving sister, Diane (who lectures on the healing power of humor), and my sister-in-law, Joan, have bridged great distances with bonds of love and support.

A quartet of painter friends were steadfast and helpful: Tony Bechara, Irving Petlin, John Moore, and Robert Berlind. My cousin, the award-winning sculptor, Virginia Gunter, has been a constant source of support and inspiration. Fireside talks in their Millbrook home with Samuel Shaw and his wife, Elizabeth, formerly of the Museum of Modern Art and Christie's, have always refreshed my spirit.

Axel Röhm has been an astute and faithful collector of my work, and he and his wife, Patrizia, have been stalwart friends.

In France, my personal legion of honor and thanks go to Jacques de Jouffroy, Caroline Bouchart, Vera Röhm, and Heinz Peter Schwerfel, with bouquets to Francine Rieu, Ann Cremin, Don Foresta, Horst Haack, Ralph Jacob, Chloe Aaron, Caroline Bissière, Pierre de Rohan-Chabot, Thierry St. Clivier, and Bernard Pivot, host of the television series *Bouillon de Culture*, who, on the occasion of my first Paris exhibition, invited me to parade my paintings and my French on his popular program.

Critics, art historians, and writers on art have been encouraging, including Eleanor Heartney, Irving and Lucy Sandler, Betsy Baker, Robert Rosenblum, Barbara Novak, Brian O'Doherty, and Paul Cummings. Arthur C. Danto has honored me by putting my paintings on the covers of three of his books and by writing a foreword for this one. Joan Marter has a special place in my heart as the first to remark on my work in print, while Manuel Jover and John Paoletti have also written perceptively and generously. The artist Kim Keever has photographed my work for years with exemplary care.

I've been heartened by the friendship and support of Marion Connor, Irving and Greta Rothman, Gale Hansen, Peter Bradley, Harry Nasse, Bill Viola, Nam June Paik, Benny Andrews, Barbara Westman, Paul Zelanski, George Chaplin, John Coplans, Jane Farver, Lee Savage, Georges and Ann Borchardt, Lloyd and Anne Moss, Elizabeth Ginzberg, Bill Davis, Maryellen Klein, Dale Riehl, Varujan Boghosian, Joseph McQuillan, Bernard Chaet, Tom Armstrong, Joy Jacobs, Flora and Sydney Biddle, Mary Etherington, Louisa McIntosh, Nat Johnson, Michio Ihara, Molly Barnes, Geoffrey Leven, Nadine Covert, Lee Lorenz, Ann Woodward, Marcia Spires, Brendan Gill, Sanford Wurmfeld, Arnold and Caroline Roth, and Cathie Curran.

A special bow to Peter Ackroyd and Roberta Scimone of Journey Editions for their trust in me, and to Lelia Ruckenstein, whose editing has championed clarity and spared the reader some tangled and interminable sentences. Thanks to Isabelle Bleecker for her grace, skill, and humor in guiding this to completion.

My most heartfelt thanks goes to Adele Stroh, whose love, charm, intelligence, and extraordinary good humor have guided me, and been a solace to my soul, ever since these paintings began. I consider myself blessed with good fortune, and my friends know its deepest source. If credit for these paintings should rightly be shared with others, move over, Manet and Rembrandt, and make room for Adele.

The Marx Brothers at the Louvre

I recall a day when a rather eminent social historian came to a party in my studio. He was bearded and burly and, I thought, a bit grumpy, as he stalked from painting to painting without saying a word. At last, he walked up to me and growled, "It's the Marx Brothers at the Louvre!" With the possible exception of my cartoonist friends, I don't know any artists who would be cheered by such a pronouncement. To me, it was the most exalted compliment I had ever received.

Artists (as well as poets, writers, architects, composers, and the like) have been copying the work of earlier artists since art began. Usually it reflects their admiration or their eagerness to absorb the style and technique of a master, either to develop their own art upon a firm base or to inherit the master's success by emulating his or her "look." On a practical level, artists have used bits and pieces of older works—from a particular pose or grouping of figures to entire compositions. Sometimes the quotation is deliberately obvious, intended to be recognized by a sophisticated audience as being, simultaneously, a tribute to an artist of the past and a staking out of new territory. Chinese scholar-painters of the Ch'ing dynasty would make paintings assembled from fragments of various masters, throw a party, and invite their colleagues to puzzle out their origins over copious servings of tiger-bone wine. The nineteenth-century French artist Edouard Manet, generally acclaimed as a dominant figure in the beginnings of modern art, copied, quoted, and made daring adaptations of the work of artists he admired.

The Marx Brothers were my heroes long before I heard of Manet and those other great artists in whose shadow I now work and play. In the thirties, the Regent Theatre in Arlington, Massachusetts, was my Louvre, my Opéra, and my Panthéon. The guide to that magic world was a small, courtly, retired traveling salesman who wore old-fashioned wing-tip collars and walked, cane in hand, with a sort of dignified shuffle. He sported a gray fedora, a dandy little white moustache, and smoked inexpensive cigars called White Owl. John F. Connor himself, if you please. The three grandsons with whom he lived, together with our parents, worshipped him and called him Gramps. He took us to the movies every Saturday afternoon. He was a beloved town character and as funny as anyone on the silver screen. If I blame those marvelous, interminable afternoons for tilting me early in life toward fantasy over reality, Gramps must share with Groucho and company some responsibility for my shameless desire to make people laugh. Even as I missed the grown-up punch lines, I could hear, when he spoke to his cronies in front of Grant's department store, that words were a grander toy than anything in Santa's bag. I could see the light in their eyes when he took someone's tired phrase, gave it a little twist, and then twirled it again, leaving it still dancing around in everyone's head after he was half way down the block, slow as he was. "I'm movin' slow, but goin' fast." I learned that humor could be a cure for what ails you, a shield against the local barbarians, and a Trojan horse, bearing truth that can't get in the gate on its own.

What have I done now, I wonder, but translate elements of Gramps's humor into visual terms? A couple of his jokes, told to me when I was a small child, have, in their patterns and rhythm, a striking relationship to the paintings in this book. The first has to do with setting up expectations, a plausible mental destination, and then jumping the track. "If we had some ham, we could have some ham and eggs, if we had some eggs." That was guaranteed to draw a giggle from any pre-cholesterol-era five-year-old. How old was I when I heard the second one? "What's the difference between the Prince of Wales, a monkey's father, and a bald man?" Answer: "One is the heir apparent, one is a hairy parent, and one has *no* hair apparent." I'm sure I laughed at that before I knew what an heir apparent was (Princes of Wales aren't so sure, either, apparently). Here, one starts to smile at the silliness of the juxtaposition and then is delighted by the surprise of their aural kinship. I don't think my grandfather was the author of either of those jokes, but the boldness, in one case, to undermine the familiar and, in the other, to seize wildly disparate elements and find a comic verbal link was very much part of his style (and, of course, of Groucho's). I recognize it when I see it in my painting, the constant setting up and upsetting of expectations, and the taste for a punning *visual* compatibility among the most unlikely partners.

How I came to choose those unlikely partners, plucking them outright from the pages of art history, is another question whose answer can be found in my personal history, which includes fifteen years working in art museums. It would be pleasant to think that my paintings are rewarding to look at on their own, but paintings are never on their own, and these are carrying a lot of freight. The autobiographical sources of my work, as much as I understand them, are suggested here and throughout the book. The art historical references are given with each painting. Together with originality, the role of humor in art is an issue that hovers over these pages, and I have been astonished at the depth of feeling it can provoke.

"I have a rule," said the art critic Robert Pincus-Witten, disdaining the work of a contemporary sculptor known for his playful wit, "if it's funny, it's not art!"

"But you say you like *my* work," I replied, in some confusion.

"Ah, but your painting is not *funny*. That's your problem."

The conversation was interrupted and never resumed. I was left to assume that my work would be embraced more warmly by the New York art world if I could dress it in somber threads of theory, with earnest discussion of strategies, irony, deconstruction, simulation, decoding, transgression, and the function of cultural myths in representation. Alas, I've spent my life in flight from earnest people, and it's unlikely I'm going to join their ranks now. I prefer the club-sandwich theory of art, proposed by the painter Robert Berlind on visiting my studio for the first time.

"I like the humor in your work."

"Thanks very much," I said, "but I like to think there's a serious level underneath the humor."

"Ah," he exclaimed, "I see *that*, too, and underneath that there's another funny level."

It surely is a sign of *gravitas* deficiency ("Gravity," said Montesquieu, "is the happiness of imbeciles.") that I recall the education of my funny bone better than I can remember school learning. After my grandfather, my best companion in laughter was my older brother Bob. While the eldest, Roy, was off to war, and much of the world was in combat or mortal danger, Bob and I would fall down laughing reading aloud to each other from Leacock, Thurber, Benchley, Perelman, and Wodehouse. We discovered the silent mastery of Buster Keaton, and cartoons in *The New Yorker* replaced comic books. I began drawing cartoons while sitting in the back of classrooms and graduated from class comedian to yearbook cartoonist.

The idea of art school was not greeted with huzzahs by my father. To be fair, the annual number of huzzahs hurled into the air in that part of the world by fathers rejoicing in a son's proposal to spend his life prancing about in a beret and paint-covered smock was rather low. An exchange between my parents, overheard as I paused at the top of the stairs, was of the sort that aspiring, angst-driven young artists might welcome when their store of self-pity runs low. Father: "Where did this artist stuff come from? We've never had anything like it in my family." Mother: "I don't remember ever hearing of anything like this, either" (conveniently overlooking her niece, Virginia Gunter, already in art school and now a highly regarded sculptor). I'm sure I bore a brooding resemblance to a martyred saint for weeks after that, inwardly moved that I was joining a noble line of great artists who had been scorned and misunderstood, and I hadn't even gotten to *art school* yet.

Eventually I went to two art schools. When I graduated from the Massachusetts College of Art in 1950, I had acquired a permanent fascination with the art and artists of nineteenth-century France and an academic, diluted Impressionist technique for painting figures and landscape. This came in handy during the Korean War, when I convinced the Navy I could do less harm to my country as a combat artist than as a distracted clerk in Navy headquarters in Tokyo (I have a recurring vision of a destroyer with a skeleton crew that hasn't been paid since 1951). I was given remarkable freedom to go back and forth to Korea, where I made sketches and took photos that I later worked up into paintings for the Navy archives. The training in copying photographs would later be useful when I began copying the masters. The best work I did in Korea was a series of drawings of Korean orphans, their faces sometimes reminding me that my countrymen had been there since 1945.

In Japan, I fell in love with the country and with a lovely young woman named Toshiko.

The respect that the Japanese offered simply because one announced oneself as an artist was a revelation to me. The heart-stopping beauty of Kyoto, Nara, and Ise contributed to the feeling that, as an artist, I had come home. We were married in 1953, and the following year I completed my Navy tour in Japan. My painting was beginning to change dramatically under the influence of modern Japanese calligraphy. The sheer, expressive power of broad, black ink strokes soaked into white rice paper, illegible even to most Japanese, suddenly struck down my resistance to abstraction. The year 1955 was distinguished by the birth of a handsome, sweet-tempered boy, Daniel (Dan is also a Japanese name), and my first exhibition, in Tokyo, as an abstract painter. We returned to the United States at the end of the year to start chasing the master's degree that I would need to sustain a family by teaching art on a college level. I also knew I had a lot to learn.

Then, as now, I believed that a great art school depended on a great artist teacher, and Josef Albers at Yale towered over the field. A veteran of the Bauhaus, where he had taught alongside Wassily Kandinsky and Paul Klee, Albers taught a famous color course at Yale that "opened eyes" for thousands of artists and architects. He invited as visiting artists New York Abstract Expressionists whose style was diametrically opposed to that of his own geometric color paintings, as long as they had "integrity." Since he saw my calligraphic style in 1956 as an attempt to be trendy ("the great vuns ver never on the bandvagon"), we tangled frequently that first year. Most of the nineteenth-century French artists I admired had fought with their teachers, so I confess with some embarrassment that I ended with the highest grade that he ever gave to a painting student at Yale. That was soon topped, in July of 1958, with the birth of our enchanting little girl, Amy (Emi, as in Emiko, has the same root as the word for "beautiful" in Japanese).

After teaching a few years at the University of Rhode Island, the intercession of a French friend working at Air France and a grant from an obscure foundation in Ohio brought me at last to Paris. Since those heady days, I've been fortunate to spend long periods of my life in France, hoping to shed my early infatuation and develop a more worldly, cynical attitude toward its charms and its failings. But the land, the language, the culture, and the friends I have made there hold me ever deeper in spiritual and sentimental allegiance. In 1962, while hip young Parisians were excited about the Nouvelle Vague cinema, I must have seemed a dated caricature of the foreign artist discovering Paris, walking the streets of Montmartre and Montparnasse in a romantic reverie, evoking the ghosts of my heroes, savoring the exhilarating air of their genius. As I haunted the galleries, the Louvre, and the Jeu de Paume, I at least knew that I could not go back to their time or see life as they saw it and that only academic and kitsch artists mimicked the styles of an earlier age. I was going to be an artist of my own time.

Although the abstract style I had developed bore the marks of my admiration for Asian art, Abstract Expressionism, and the Parisian artist Nicholas de Staël, I considered it my duty, as an artist, to find my own voice, to express my own personality, to create something that had not previously existed. And I never doubted that art was a profoundly serious endeavor.

What happened upon my return from Paris to shake those comfortable assumptions was the impact of a large box that fits in everybody's home. The shattering effect on my painting of entering the world of television in 1963, first as host of a weekly program from the Museum of Fine Arts, Boston, is recounted in the following pages. It was an immersion that lasted through the seventies, as I continued to produce, write, and narrate programs about art for public and cable television. Painting nearly stopped until I went to France at the end of the decade to spend some months painting still lifes and portraits—as if beginning again. Then, astonishingly, in the eighties, as director of education at the Whitney Museum of American Art, while producing award-winning films and videos about its collection, exhibitions, and biennials, my painting revived vigorously. It could no longer be a lyrical, abstract reverie about color. I had come to realize that art as diffused (or confused) through the media could *itself* become a subject for art. This brought a playful spirit that my grandfather might have recognized into my work for the first time.

The humor in these paintings is, for me, without mockery. The risk in mixing mirth and the masters is that it will be perceived as making fun of *them*. These artists have been my heroes, my teachers, my monsters, and my landscape. I have no illusion of actually matching their skill. The recommended viewing distance for my paintings is three thousand miles from the originals. Whether or not I have understood the depth of their achievement, they are as familiar to me, and as loved, as the flowers in Monet's garden were to him. If I am making fun of anything, it is of us, of mass culture, of what we, with the best of intentions, have done in the name of the democratization, and the commercialization, of art and technology. Whatever liberties I have taken with these marvelous images, they are reverential compared to what is already happening as students begin playing with the treasures of the Louvre, the Metropolitan Museum, and the National Gallery on CD-ROM. They have a great opportunity to study how art is put together. Maybe these pages will encourage them to approach the past with respect as well as humor.

A word may be in order here about the technique employed in making these paintings. The classic method for copying a picture by hand is the same as that used to transfer a small drawing to a large canvas. Both the art reproduction to be copied and the canvas are squared off in a grid, and the artist builds his copy square by square. I rejected this proven, rational method as too boring, and for the first few years I copied the hard way, that is, freehand, squinting at the small reproduction of a masterpiece as if it were a model at the far end of the room, mentally enlarging it as I painted it on the canvas. One day it dawned on me that, considering the vastness of the moral wasteland I had entered on becoming a pirate, the use of a simple slide projector to trace the outlines of figures was not likely to condemn me to a lower order of perdition. I soon discovered that two projectors were even better. I could move two paintings around on the canvas, enlarging or reducing them until I found the invisible line where they could be joined as seamlessly as possible. Then I would trace simple outlines with a brush on a toned canvas in the darkness and, lights on, begin to build the painting from printed reproductions—the larger and truer in color, the better. All this, of course, would appear quite slow and primitive to a computer graphic artist, indifferent to the sensuous delights of manipulating oil paint.

It seems to me quite fitting that paintings that were derived from reproductions now find their way back to the printed page. The original masterpieces are still intact in their museums and private collections, serene and indifferent in their quiet splendor to the reckless cavorting of their printed offspring. For me, the experience has been more than a journey back in time or a chance to commune with some of my heroes. ("What do you think you're *doing*, boy?" was a question shared by many of them.)

This is a story of an artist who had nearly thrown in the brushes and palette. Somehow I was given a second chance, heartened by the encouragement of dear friends, finding inspiration in the past and in that much abused medium, television, that had long ago lured me away from my studio. I hope the reader will sense, and share, the awakening pleasure and gratitude that will always fill these paintings for me, and enjoy a strolling, leisurely tour through my fantasy museum.

The Plates

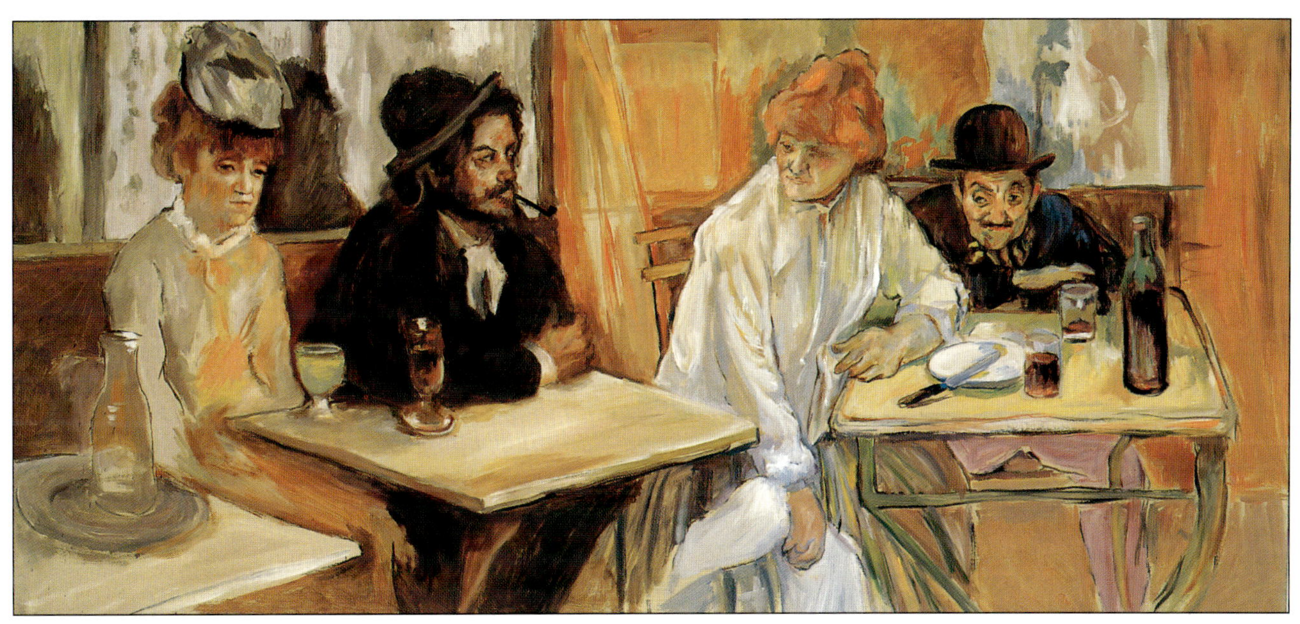

The Spanish Hat Trick

1964, 40 x 30 inches

Source

El Greco, *Portrait of Covarrubias,* 1600, Louvre, Paris

My quiet career as an abstract painter was interrupted in 1963 when I became the host of a weekly TV program, *Museum Open House*, broadcast from the Museum of Fine Arts in Boston. The half-hour, black-and-white series was produced by the museum together with WGBH, broadcast after Julia Child in Boston and New York, and later viewed around the country. For the next four years, I was astonished to find myself an instant expert on the art of the world (we called it "Museum Open Mouth" around my house). I usually chose subjects that I wanted to study—one week, Spanish painting; the next, Rembrandt, Egyptian sculpture, African art, or Japanese woodblock prints.

It was fascinating to see what happened to art when it was squeezed, stretched, drained of color, and sent into thousands of homes in the form of electronic pulses. Condensing the complexities of art history into a half-hour script was an impossible task, but I enjoyed writing and performing. My own painting output, not surprisingly, declined sharply. In desperation, I tried to deal with this strange new life on canvas. What emerged is this El Greco portrait as if seen on TV, the camera apparently tilting down while at the same time something drastic is happening to the vertical control. The title of the work was inspired by the momentary illusion of a hat appearing at the top of the painting.

I put this and a few related works aside as not being serious and returned to being a part-time abstract painter. I was drawn further into the production of films and video about art and was attracted to the idea of video itself as an art form. In the early eighties, in the process of reviving my life as a painter, I literally took this painting out of the closet. It struck me that its media-skewed view of art described a phenomenon of our time, the popularization of culture, that had nearly engulfed my life. The flood of art appreciation courses and reproductions of art masterpieces, together with the romanticization of artists' lives in movies, has left everyone with a shifting, half-remembered, muddled mental museum. I was suddenly consumed with the desire to explore this fantasy museum in my studio.

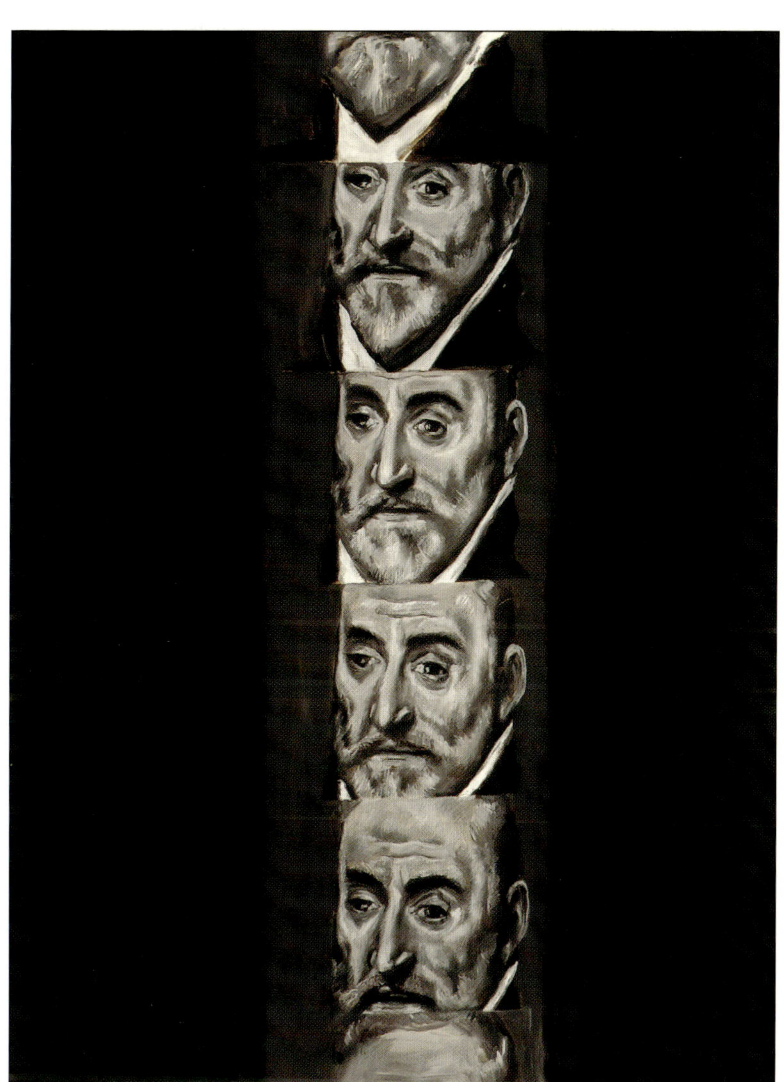

Roll Over, Rembrandt

1982, 60 x 48 inches

Source

Rembrandt, *Self-Portrait* (detail), 1655, Kunsthistoriches Museum, Vienna

In what might have appeared to an observer as a demented state, I took a large, abandoned abstraction and copied a Rembrandt self-portrait smack in the middle. I repeated it and sat staring at this bizarre apparition, startled but invigorated. By imposing a rough image of the seventeenth-century master on top of an abstract work, I had joined two styles that were incompatible spatially, aesthetically, philosophically, and historically.

In an exaggerated form, it graphically depicted the central division in the art of our time and in my own training—figurative vs. abstract. Like most artists of the period, my early training had been figurative. "It's OK to be an artist," said my father, "if you can paint like Rembrandt." The figurative tradition in my painting department at the Massachusetts College of Art held Rembrandt in great esteem but had "advanced" to a late, academic Impressionism. Primarily based on painting still life and the nude model, it was taught by a witty Irishman named Patrick Gavin, who lamented that too much copying of the masters in his youth had stunted his originality as an artist. The Impressionists, with their heroic, communal struggle in the face of scorn and ridicule, became my idols, alongside Rembrandt and Daumier. I knew little of an ongoing struggle in New York, where the Abstract Expressionists were about to win international recognition for American art.

My abrupt, miraculous conversion to abstract painting came a few years later in Japan, under the influence of modern calligraphy, and it was confirmed at Yale's School of Fine Arts under the guidance of the Bauhaus colorist Josef Albers ("Connor, you're not Japanese!"). I became a true believer and, I think, a good abstract painter, but I realize now that vaulting over the previous ninety years of art history had left me concerned about the foundation of my work. You must go *through* Cubism, someone had said. If I had been on firmer ground, perhaps I wouldn't have been so readily diverted to extolling the masters on television or, with this painting, twenty years later, so willing to push abstraction into the background again to travel once more to the time of my heroes.

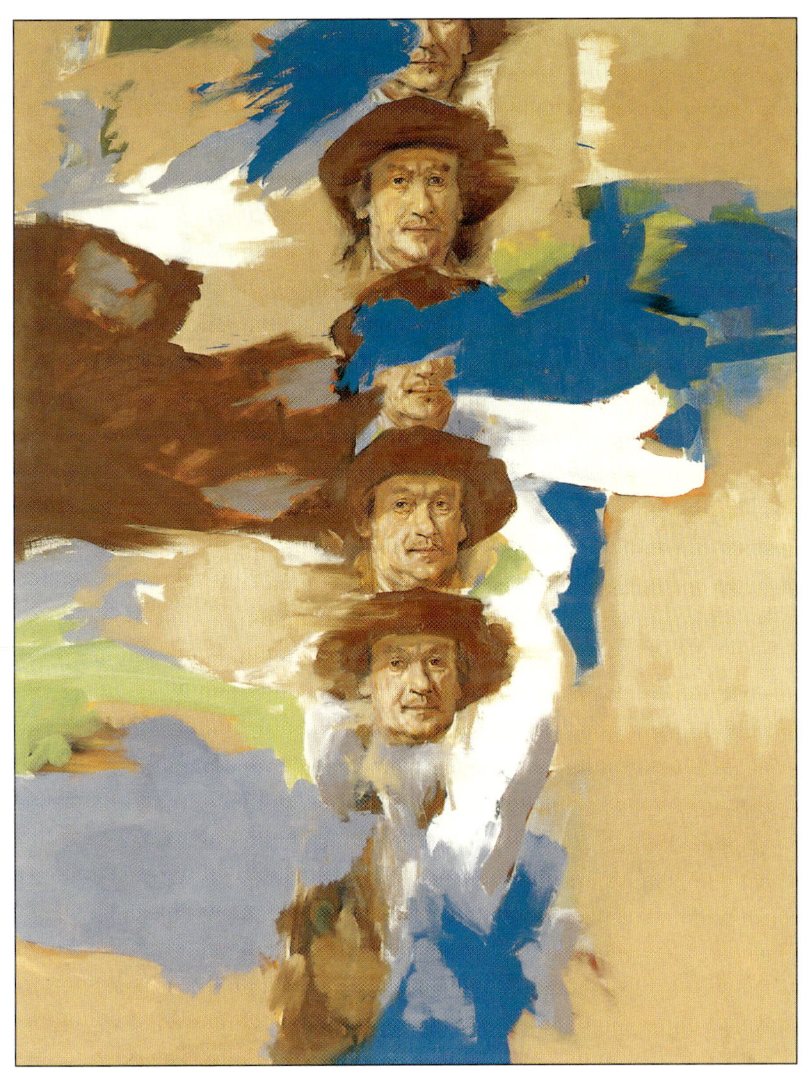

Rise and Shine

1983, 48 x 60 inches

Source

Michelangelo, *Creation of Adam* (detail), 1508–12, The Vatican, Rome

Although a child could have advised me against it, I tried a few more times to integrate the masters with abstract painting. This one suggests that the Creation of Adam took place in severe atmospheric turbulence. I knew *I* was in heavy weather. Trying to avoid the look of a traditional image pasted on top of an abstraction, or compartmentalizing the two styles side by side, I tried to bring them along together, hoping that some interaction might be generated. Obviously, for that to happen I would have had to expressively distort the Michelangelo, as Picasso felt free to adapt Velasquez to his own style in his variations on *The Maids of Honor*. I felt it was important to try to respect the appearance of the original, to keep it recognizable. Pablo could play around with the masters all he wanted; some of us know enough to keep our distance.

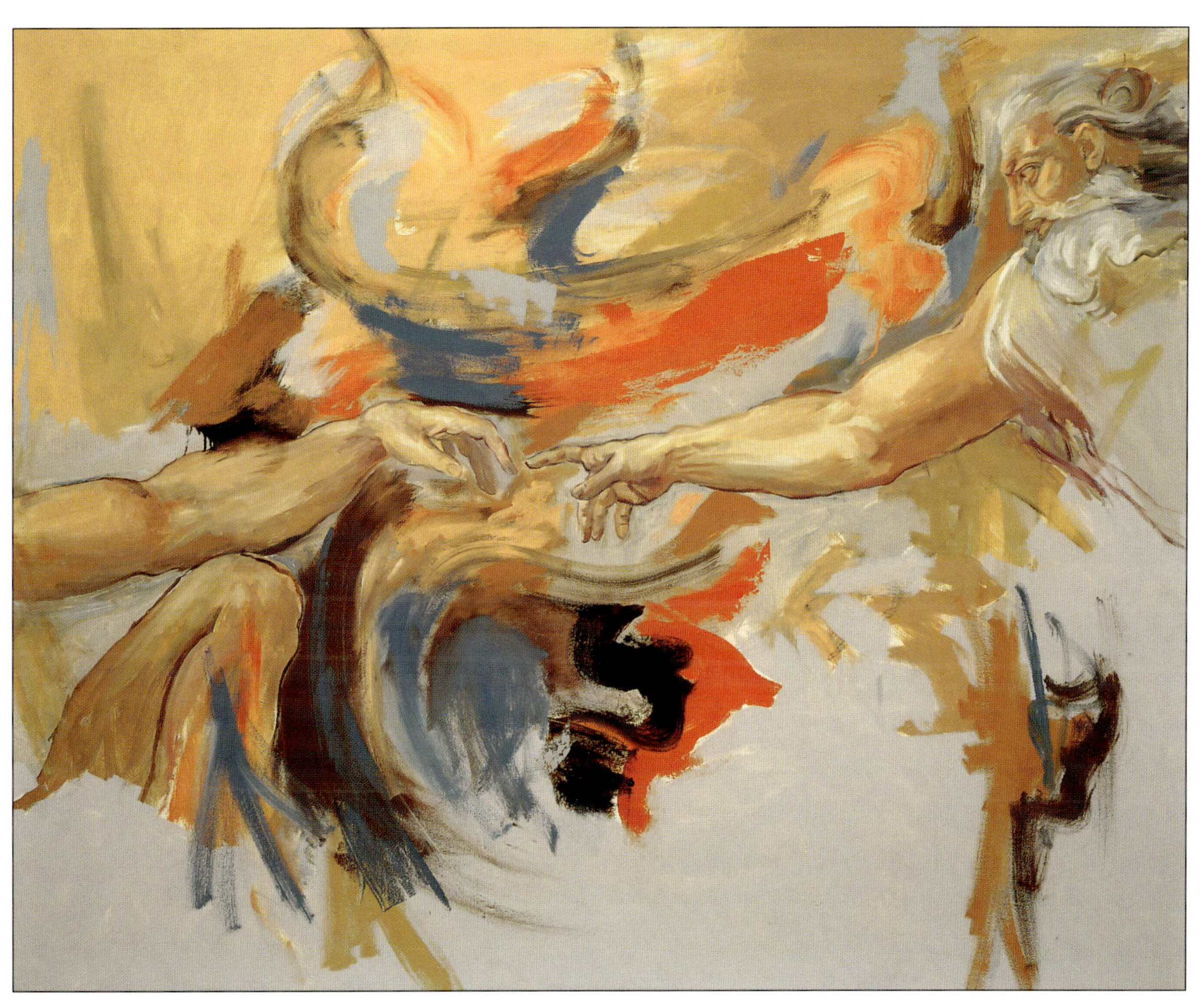

Cultivate Your Garden I

1984, 50 x 50 inches

Sources

Monet, *Garden at Vétheuil,* 1880,
National Gallery of Art, Washington, D.C.

Toulouse-Lautrec, *At the Moulin Rouge,* 1892,
Musée d'Orsay, Paris

Photo: Toulouse-Lautrec in his studio, 1890

As a young artist I worked as a night watchman in the Fogg Art Museum at Harvard. Alone in the galleries at three o'clock in the morning, spooked by the moving shadows of sculpture thrown against the wall by my flashlight (Rodin's striding, life-size *John the Baptist* got my attention), it wasn't hard to imagine figures from one masterpiece stepping out to visit their neighbors in a nearby painting, cherishing a stolen moment of freedom. That fantasy came freshly to mind as I began now to explore a dreamlike interactivity on canvas, abandoning all vestiges of abstraction and drawing on my experience with the moving image. In the movies of my childhood, actors often played scenes in front of rear-screen film projections that made it appear as if they were in traffic, at sea, or in the desert. The TV version was called chroma key, an electronic masking technique by which one could drop out any background and replace it with another—an anchorman in Manhattan could seem to be in Red Square. It is now the most commonplace of special effects, in movies, MTV, and video art. Artists have been creating similar effects for years with paint and collage, but it was video "magic" that directly influenced my vision as I began to remove the barriers separating my favorite art and artists.

I pored over art books in my library, beginning with my idols, the Impressionists and Post-Impressionists. A photo of Toulouse-Lautrec painting the *Moulin Rouge* in his studio and a radiant garden scene by Monet somehow came together in my mind. What if Monet, concerned that Toulouse-Lautrec's fragile health was endangered by all those nights in the smoky cabarets and dance halls of Montmartre, had invited him to paint in the fresh air of his (pre-Giverny) garden at Vétheuil? It takes a little historical juggling, but we know that such gestures were common among artists of the time. And we know that artists, if they're lucky, are obsessed; so in my painting Toulouse-Lautrec continues to paint the gang at the Moulin Rouge, oblivious to the flowers and the sound of the wind in the trees.

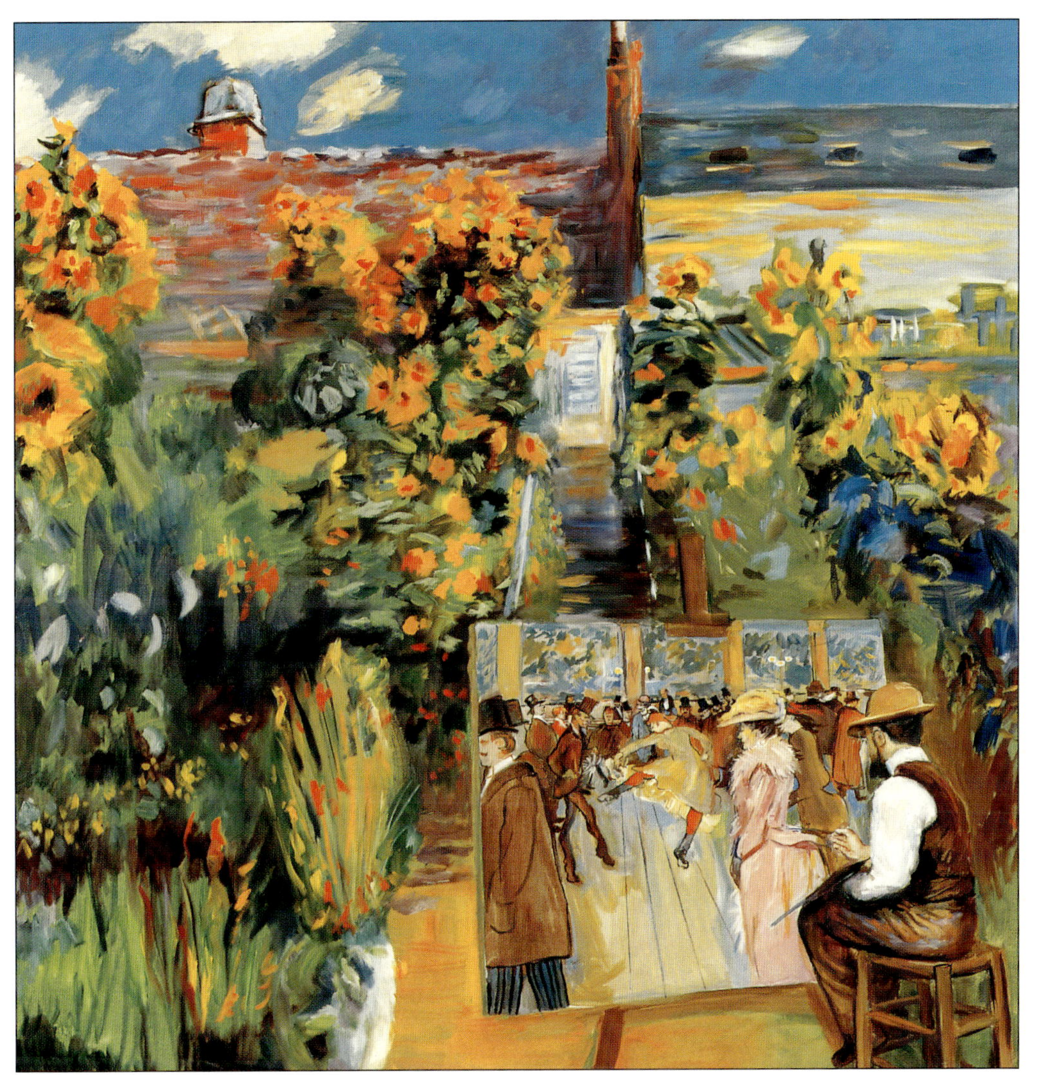

Cultivate Your Garden II

1984, 50 x 50 inches

Sources

Monet, *Garden at Vétheuil,* 1880,
National Gallery of Art, Washington, D.C.

Toulouse-Lautrec, *At the Moulin Rouge,* 1892,
Musée d'Orsay, Paris

Photo: Monet painting in his studio

A rebel from an aristocratic background, Toulouse-Lautrec was not remiss in his social obligations and would have invited Monet, in turn, to paint in the Moulin Rouge. Monet, of course, has his own passion to pursue and could not get his garden out of his thoughts. He later did paint many of his landscapes indoors, from sketches made on the scene, and once said, rather testily, "Whether my canvases are painted from life or not is nobody's business and of no importance whatsoever." It seems a curious remark from an artist who had been among the strongest, most influential voices for *plein air* painting directly from life in Impressionism's early days. Undoubtedly he had become so wise in his understanding of color in nature that he could reconstruct a landscape in his studio from sketches and notes. Eyesight problems made it easier to "read" a sketch made up close than a distant tree. In his late work, he arrived so close to the temperament of a modern abstract painter that he did not feel dependent on a literal transcription of nature to make a strong painting, and in his studio he could paint huge canvases.

Since the owner of this work has a good sense of humor, I decided to surprise him by including him among the patrons at the bar, to the right of the splendid hats.

The title, from Voltaire, also referred to my own situation. I was cultivating my vision in the gardens of others. Humor was apparently going to be a part of it, the antic view of life derived in equal parts from my grandfather and the Marx Brothers. I realized that a significant part of my personality had, for better or worse, been held back; it's difficult to express humor in abstract painting unless your name is Paul Klee.

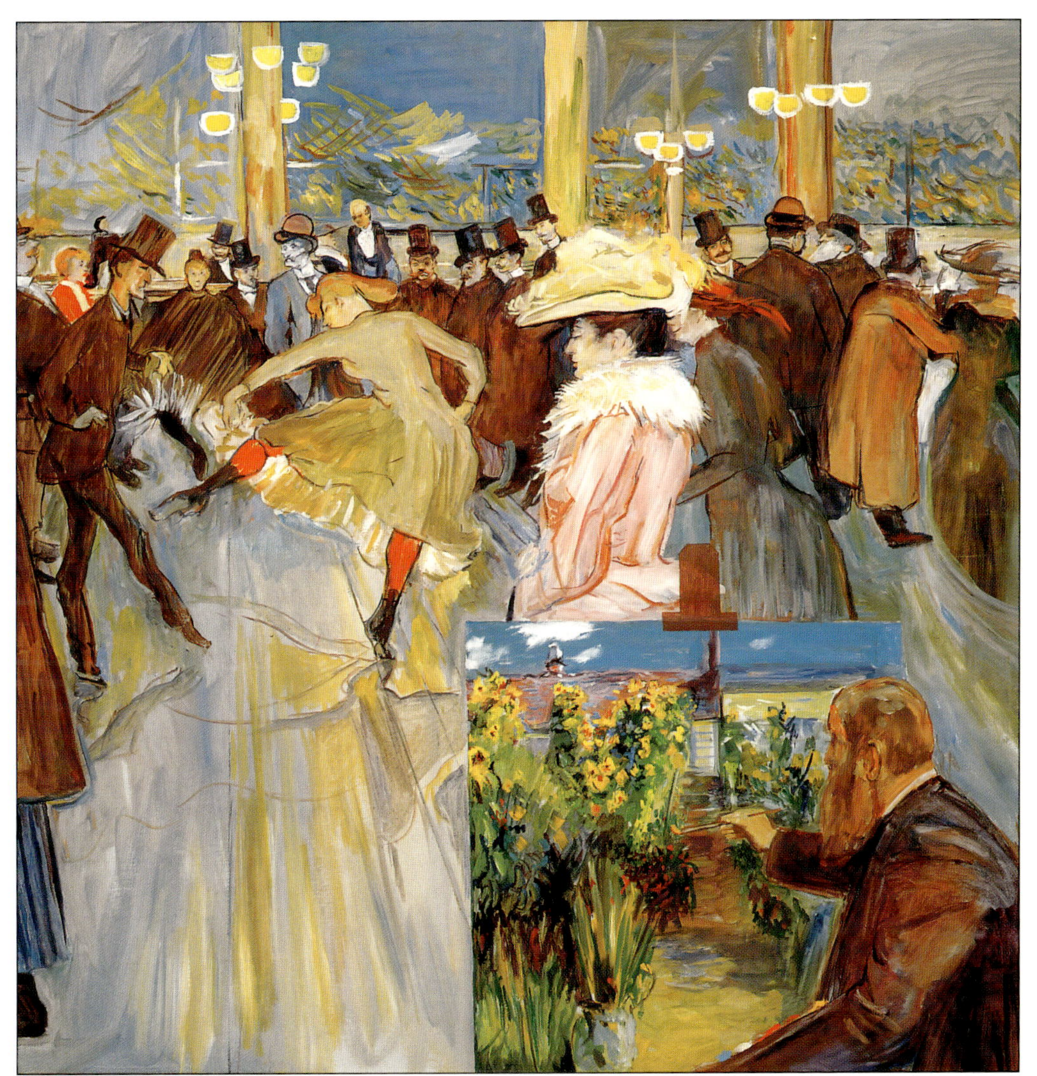

Still Life in the Old Boy I

1983, 46 x 50 inches

Sources

Cézanne, *Self-Portrait,* 1879–82, Tate Gallery, London

Cézanne, *Still Life with Apples,* 1895–98, Museum of Modern Art, New York

Eccentric as he was, why would Cézanne put a still-life painting under his arm and carry it out to one of his favorite outdoor views, of Mont Sainte-Victoire? He painted more than sixty views of the mountain from different aspects, often exaggerating its size. Distance was important to Cézanne, but it was a pictorial distance, built up by vibrations of color and direction of brushwork. The color, line, and shape of the mountain often play the same constructive role in the composition as fruit in a still life.

If you know the original of this still life in the Museum of Modern Art, you may share my wonder as to how a work can seem so unfinished and so splendidly complete at the same time. Maybe *Cézanne's* not sure either, and that's why he has taken it out of the studio to look at it in a new light. It's all right to stop after you've got the essential down, as long as you know what the essential is. That sounds like something one might encounter in a fortune cookie, but it's a problem that haunts most artists. I remember the voice of my first painting teacher, Patrick Gavin: "Connor is a model to the class in how to begin a painting." Pause, with timing of Jack Benny–like perfection. "Now, if we can only persuade him to *finish* one . . ." I told a visitor to my studio that half the works there were unfinished and that I'd sleep a lot better if I knew which half. It is a problem compounded by copying the work of great artists. I might let an unfinished *Connor* be exhibited, but I owe it to my famous colleagues to try to show them at their best.

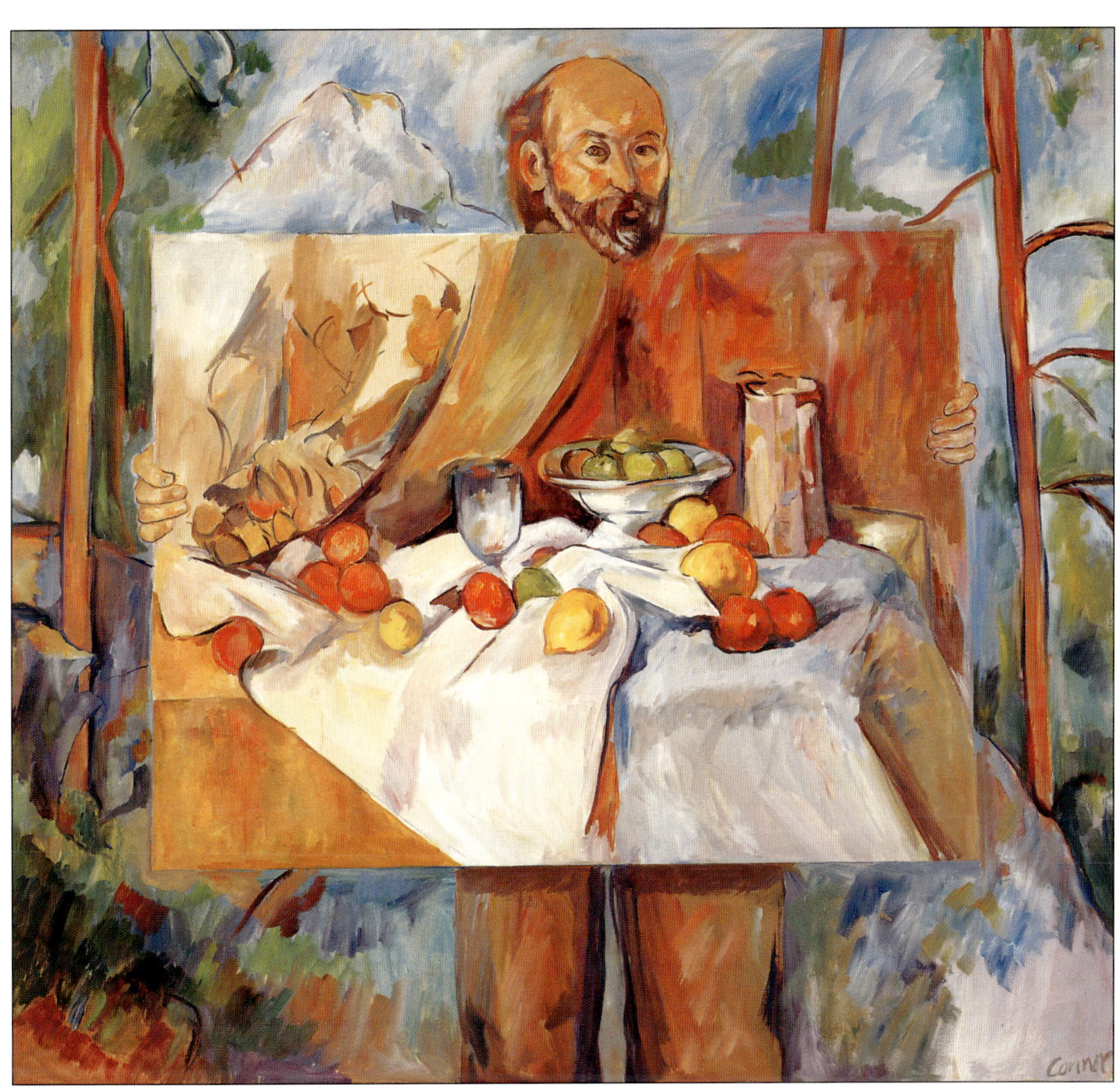
Conner

Still Life in the Old Boy II

1986, 46 x 50 inches

Sources

Cézanne, *Mont Sainte-Victoire Seen from the Bibémus Quarry,* 1898–1900, Museum of Art, Baltimore

Cézanne, *Self-Portrait* (detail, reversed), 1879–82, Kunstmuseum, Berne

Cézanne, *The Basket of Apples,* 1890–94, Art Institute of Chicago

I liked this idea well enough to do a variation, with another self-portrait and another still life. I was still wrestling with the question of how far to go in trying to replicate an original painting from a reproduction. Should I develop it just far enough to enable viewers to get the "joke," to recognize the style of the artist and perhaps the painting as well, or was it necessary to attempt the impossible, trying to copy every nuance of color and brush stroke? Visitors to the studio often liked the sketchy stage, but I pursued greater fidelity to the originals, hoping to bring them to the "double-take" point where they might ask, "What the hell is going on?" I was dependent on the size and quality of the reproduction I was copying, often cruelly clipped from a remaindered art book. Every color reproduction offers some variation on the artist's original palette, and I was beginning to imagine some future Ph.D. trying to sort out my Abrams period from my Skira. If the painting is in a New York museum, I can check out the color directly, usually alarming the guards with my close inspection.

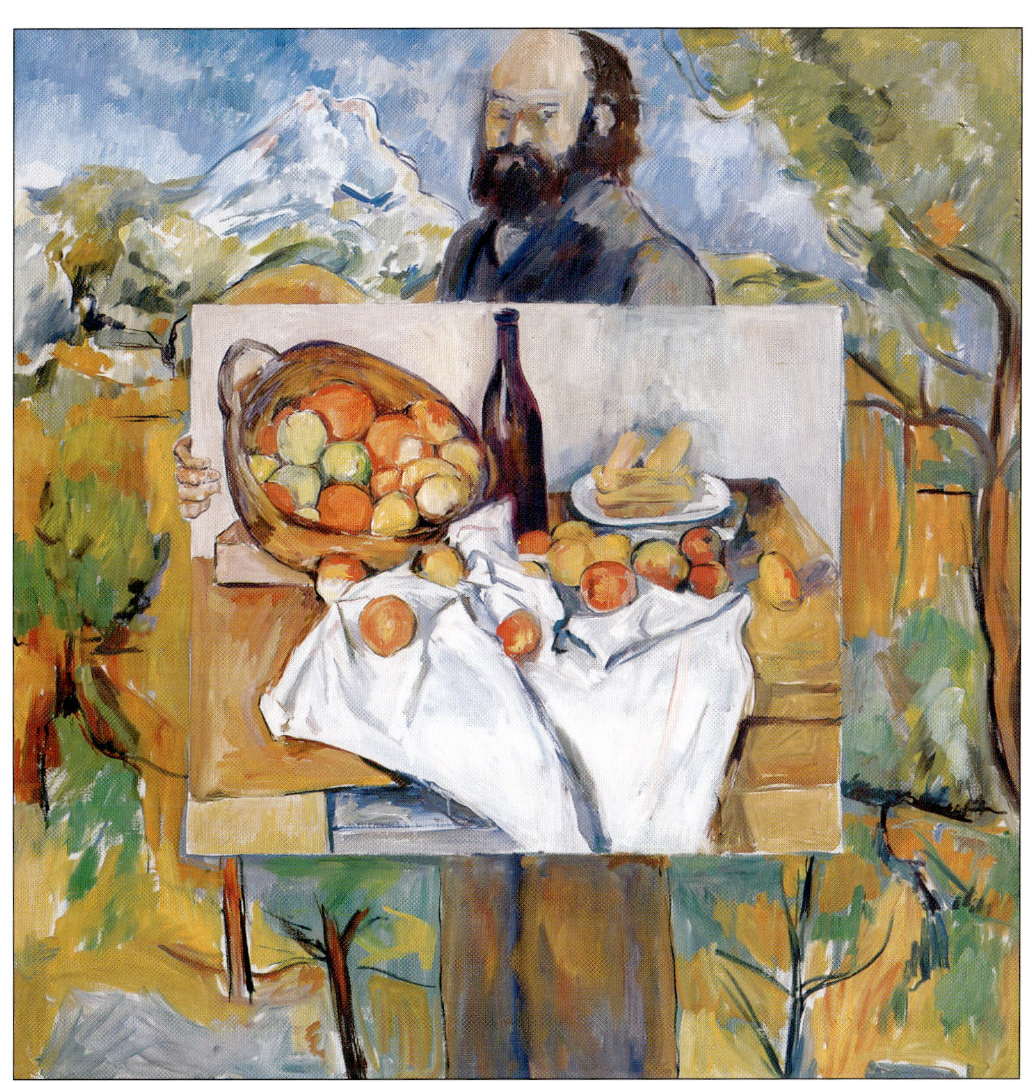

After the Fall

1984, 36 x 27 inches

Source

Degas, *The Glass of Absinthe,* 1876, Musée d'Orsay, Paris

On this occasion, I explored making small changes *within* one work, to see if I could play with its meaning without drastically altering its look. When I changed the woman's dress in *The Glass of Absinthe* from street clothes to a costume very familiar to Degas, I finally understood why she seemed dejected, seeking forgetfulness in a glass. *Something* had happened in performance; perhaps she fell down, causing such a spectacular domino effect among the corps de ballet that the stage looked like the final scene of *Hamlet,* in tutu. Her self-absorbed companion is not much help.

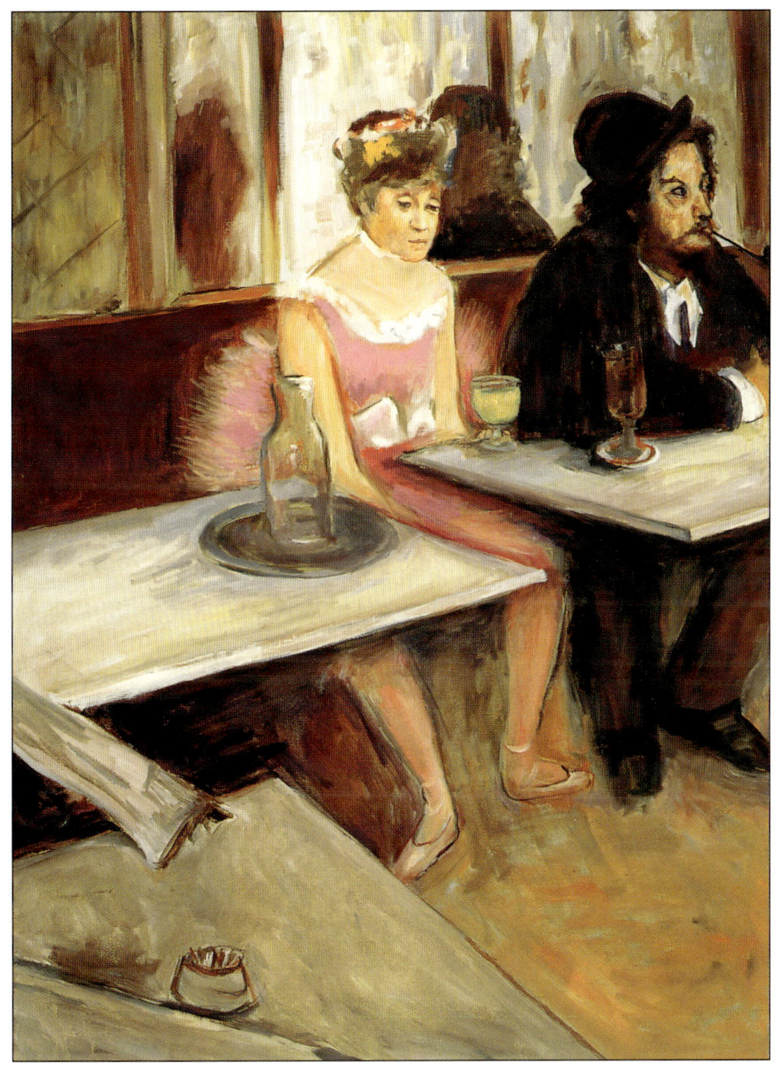

Love and Death

1984, 48 x 60 inches

Sources

Manet, *Olympia,* 1863,
Musée d'Orsay, Paris

Manet, *Dead Toreador,* 1864, National Gallery of Art, Washington, D.C.

The famous scandal provoked by Manet's *Olympia* at the Salon of 1865 was due to several breaches of Salon etiquette. The artist had recast the traditional reclining female nude, often posed in a mythological role like Venus or Danäe, with a clearly contemporary Parisian woman staring boldly at us as if welcoming a client or posing for a camera. She is attractive but unidealized, and the relatively flat modeling contributes to the immediate, graphic look of an image caught in a flash of light. If it had been a motion picture camera, directed by Alfred Hitchcock, he might have tilted down to discover a *Dead Toreador,* also by Manet. The circumstances of his demise are far from clear, but we sense she is implicated, and the aroused black cat takes on new significance.

Manet, dissatisfied with a larger bullfight painting, had cut out the toreador in the foreground and shown it separately, so I have simply attached my version of it to a different painting. Having gone this far, I had no hesitation in using a title from a Woody Allen film, in which he enjoyed a similar good time with Tolstoy and Ingmar Bergman.

In its own way, this painting had as much significance in my career as the original *Olympia* did for Manet. It seemed to validate all the searching that led up to it and to set the path for the indefinite future. It is not without irony that I was luckier with the critics than the author of the original art had been. Exhibiting in 1985 for the first time in seventeen years, in a group show called *The Art of Appropriation,* I had my work singled out by Joan Marter as "Postmodernism brilliantly exemplified." The event jolted me into recognition that I was part of a wave of artists, adrift at the apparent end of all the "isms," who had set themselves to exploring the creative uses of the past.

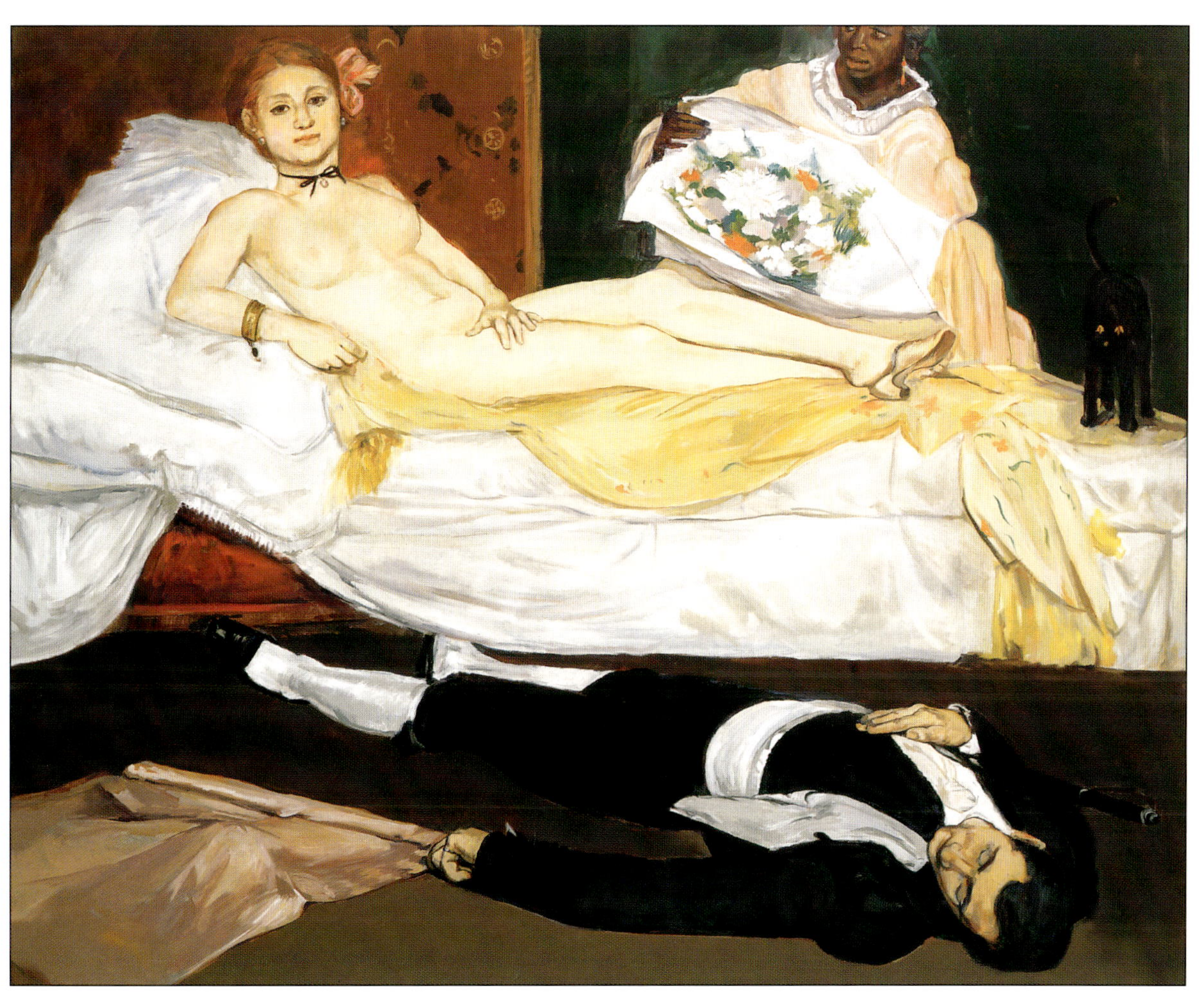

Between Poetry and Philosophy

1984, 48 x 68 inches

Sources

Rembrandt, *Aristotle Contemplating the Bust of Homer,* 1653, Metropolitan Museum of Art, New York

Rembrandt, *Bathsheba,* 1654, Louvre, Paris

Philosophy has always seemed to me a lonely job, so I offered Aristotle a little company. Contemplating the bust of the poet Homer, who lived at least three centuries before him, he perhaps gave some thought to the brevity of life and its pleasures. For a companion, I chose someone in need of wisdom, the biblical Bathsheba, contemplating a seductive offer in a letter from King David. We can assume the philosopher advised her that the path to well-being lay in the contemplative life, not in the pursuit of pleasure. On the other hand, she might have reflected on Homer's observation, "It is not possible to fight beyond your strength, even if you strive." (*The Iliad,* Book XIII, l. 787)

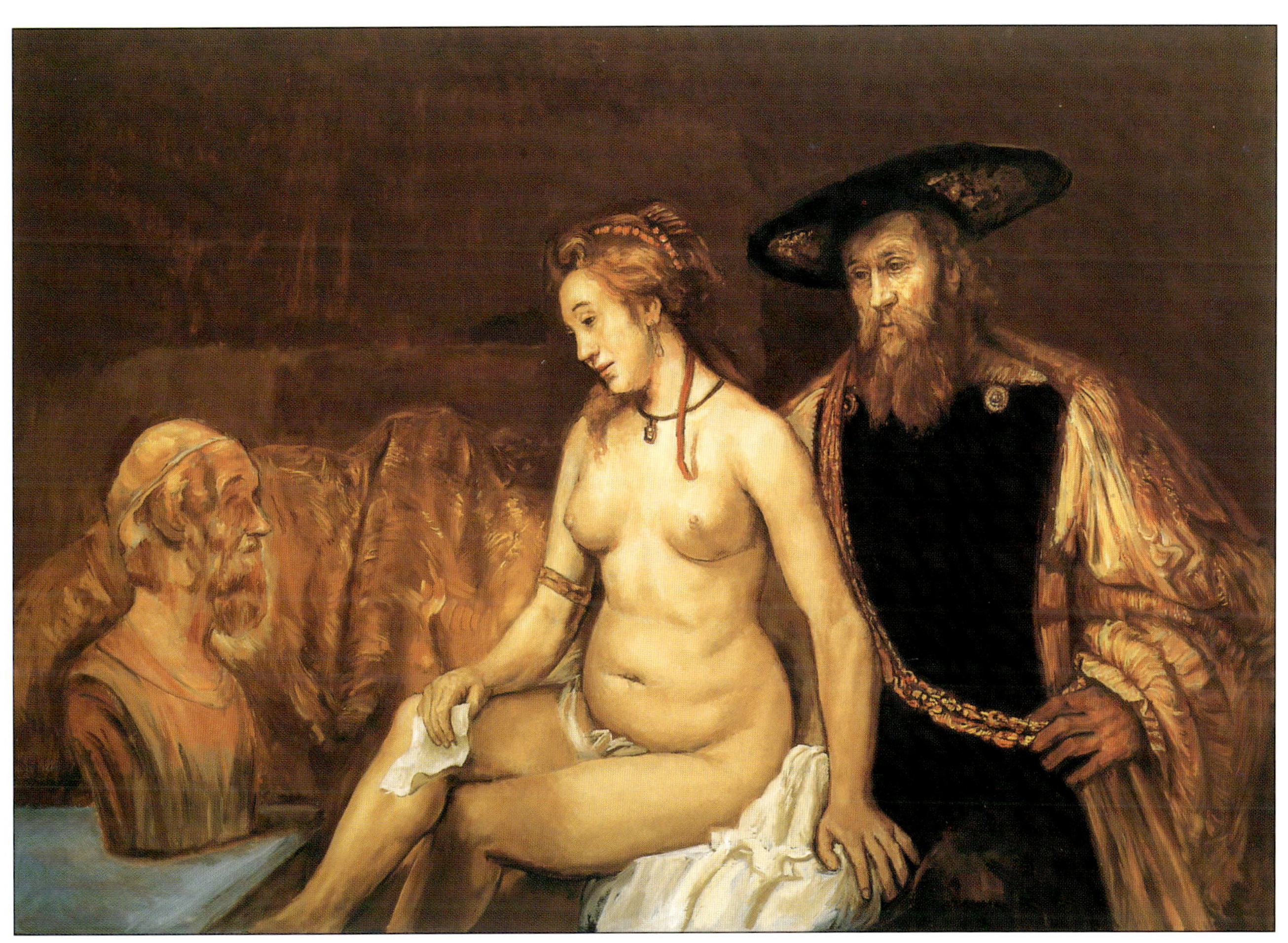

Marat/Récamier

1985, 48 x 76 inches

Sources

David, *Marat Assassinated,* 1793, Royal Museum of Fine Arts, Brussels

David, *Madame Récamier,* 1800, Louvre, Paris

Work on Jacques-Louis David's portrait of the celebrated beauty and social figure Madame Récamier was abruptly terminated when she deemed it unflattering and sought a more cooperative artist. Her *chaise longue* always looked to me like a boat, and I began to consider a companion for a little cruise down the river. The life of Marat, David's friend and a grimly vengeful leader of the French Revolution, had been abruptly terminated in his bath by Charlotte Corday, who considered him a tyrant and decided to play Brutus. My position was not unlike that of a director in the theatre, trying to cast actors in roles that depart from type and open up unexpected possibilities in each of them. The unlikely union of the revolutionary and the socialite, picnicking on the Loire at Saumur, suggests there may be an afterlife where important, unfinished lives enjoy the company of important, unfinished paintings.

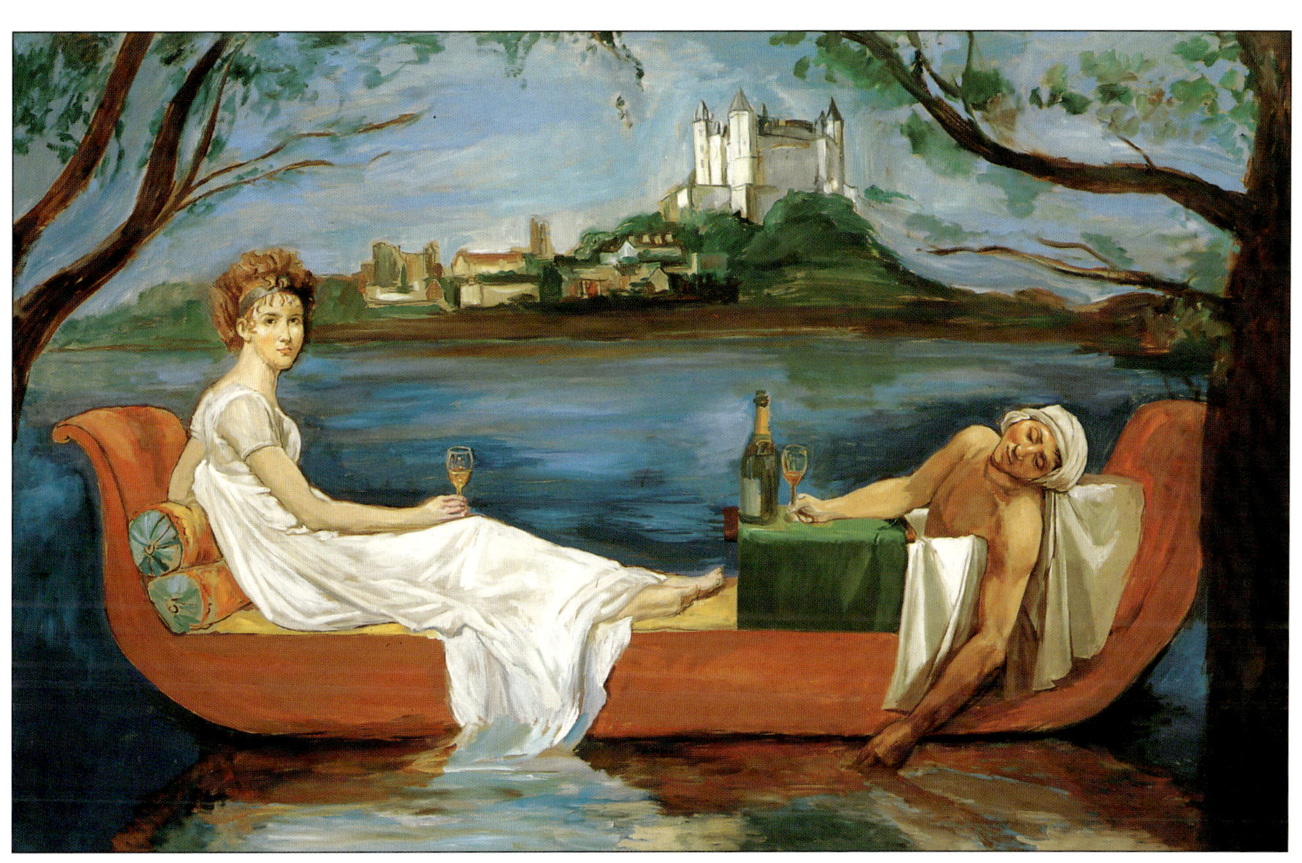

Liberation of the Harem

1985, 48 x 60 inches

Sources

Delacroix, *Liberty Leading the People,* 1830, Louvre, Paris

Ingres, *Odalisque,* 1814, Louvre, Paris

Ingres, *The Turkish Bath* (detail), 1862, Musée d'Orsay, Paris

Delacroix's *Liberty Leading the People* was a romantic hymn to revolutionary idealism, celebrating the popular uprising in Paris in 1830 that led to the downfall of the Restoration and the crowning of Louis Philippe. It was also considered an assault on the more conservative artistic traditions of his great rival of the classic school, Ingres, whose two nudes (*Odalisque*, 1814, on the left, and a detail from *The Turkish Bath*, 1862, on the right) replace, in my rough rendering, Delacroix's original foreground filled with casualties of the fighting. Here, I have tried to play a Jimmy Carter role, bringing the famous rivals together for the first, and possibly the last, time, in a worthy, feminist "Let My People Go" cause.

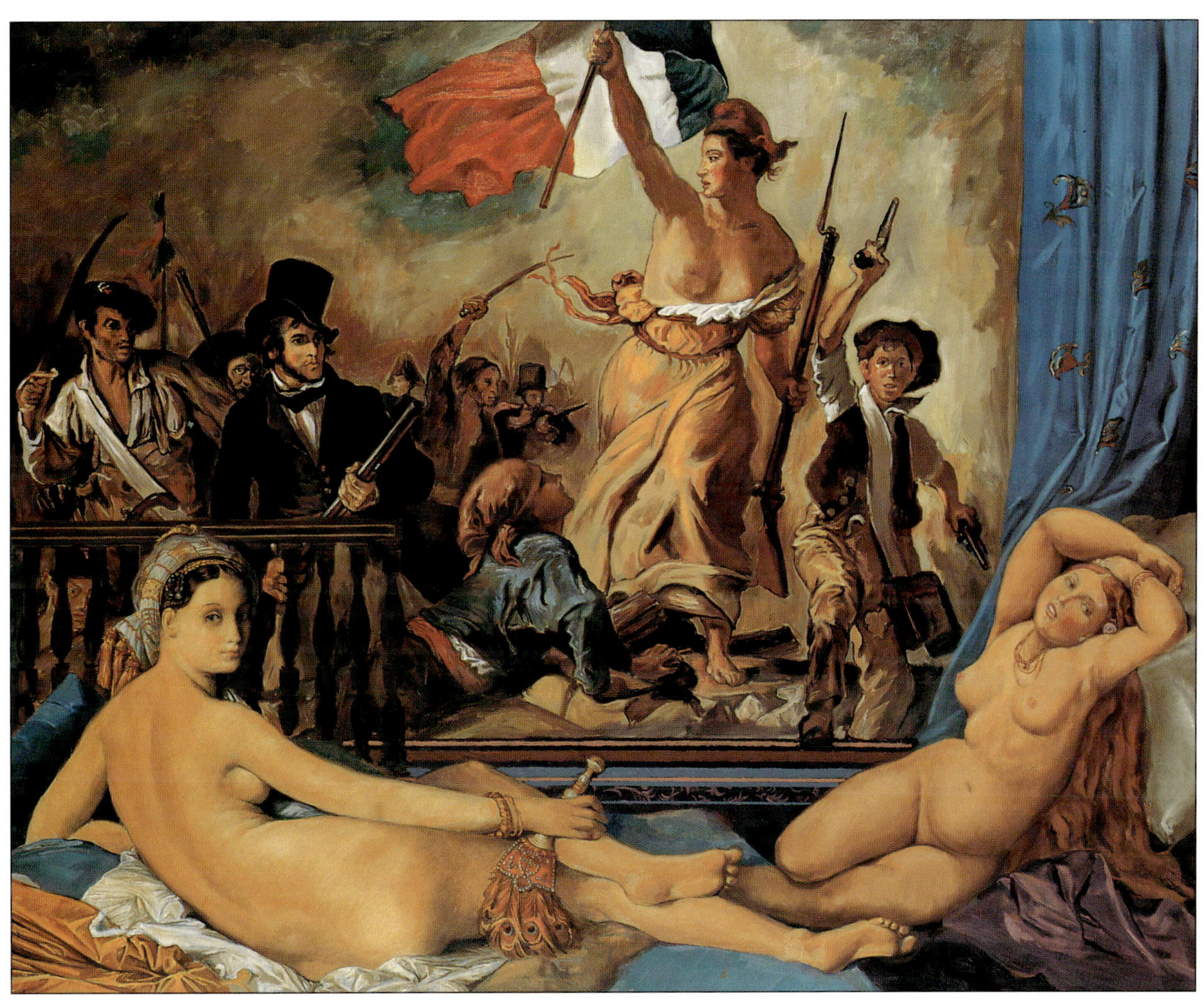

The Dawn of Modernism

1985, 48 x 60 inches

Sources

Manet, *The Execution of Maximilian,* 1867, National Gallery, London

Manet, *The Fifer,* 1867, Musée d'Orsay, Paris

Manet painted four versions of his journalistic *Execution of Maximilian*. The killing of the Austrian archduke—installed by the French as puppet emperor of colonial Mexico and then, under American pressure, abandoned to the Juaristas—shook the conscience of France. It stirred Manet to make a work sometimes confused with his hero Goya's famous *Fifth of May* execution scene. After Manet's death, his son committed another atrocity, cutting out and selling a section of the painting on which my work is based. It was later partially reconstituted by Degas. In my reassembly, Manet's *Fifer* replaces Maximilian and his two generals. Over-familiar to artists through reproductions as one of the early icons of Modernism ("I'm glad they finally got the little bastard," said one, on seeing this), the *Fifer* here represents Modernism's final moments, before its succession by Postmodernism, soon to be laid to rest in its turn.

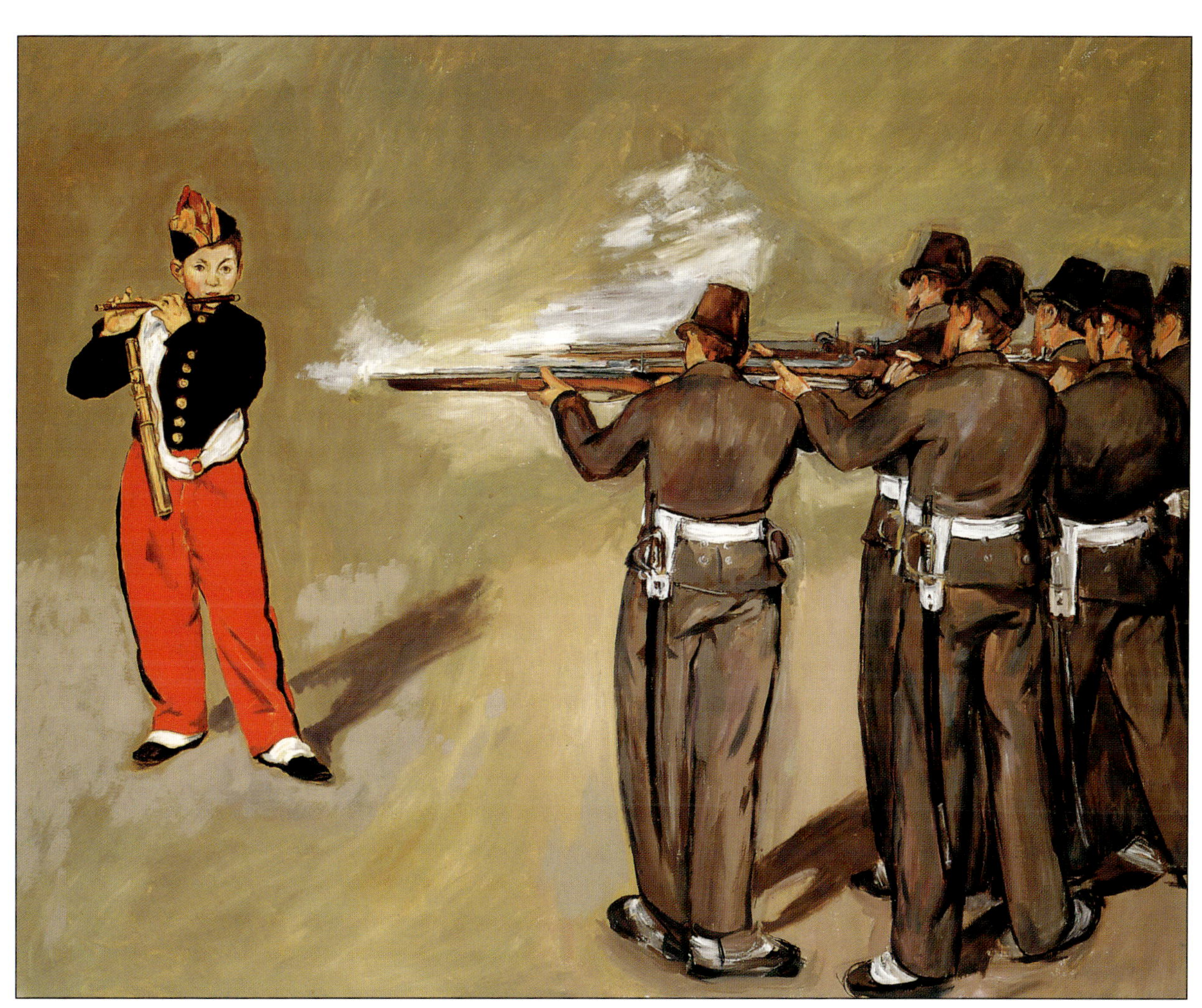

What Do Women Want?

1985, 48 x 60 inches

Sources

Rembrandt, *The Anatomy Lesson of Dr. Tulp,* 1632, Mauritshuis, The Hague

Rembrandt, *Danäe,* 1636, Hermitage, St. Petersburg

The Anatomy Lesson of Dr. Tulp, in which the famous surgeon was shown discussing the ligaments that control the fingers, was painted when Rembrandt was twenty-six and was his first major success. What else, I wondered, might the good doctors be studying so attentively? *Danäe* was originally reaching out to welcome her lover, Zeus, appearing to her disguised as a shower of gold. The title, borrowed from Freud's famous question, does not lack for answers today, but Rembrandt's doctors seem to be puzzled. Danäe herself appears to be looking beyond them for a solution.

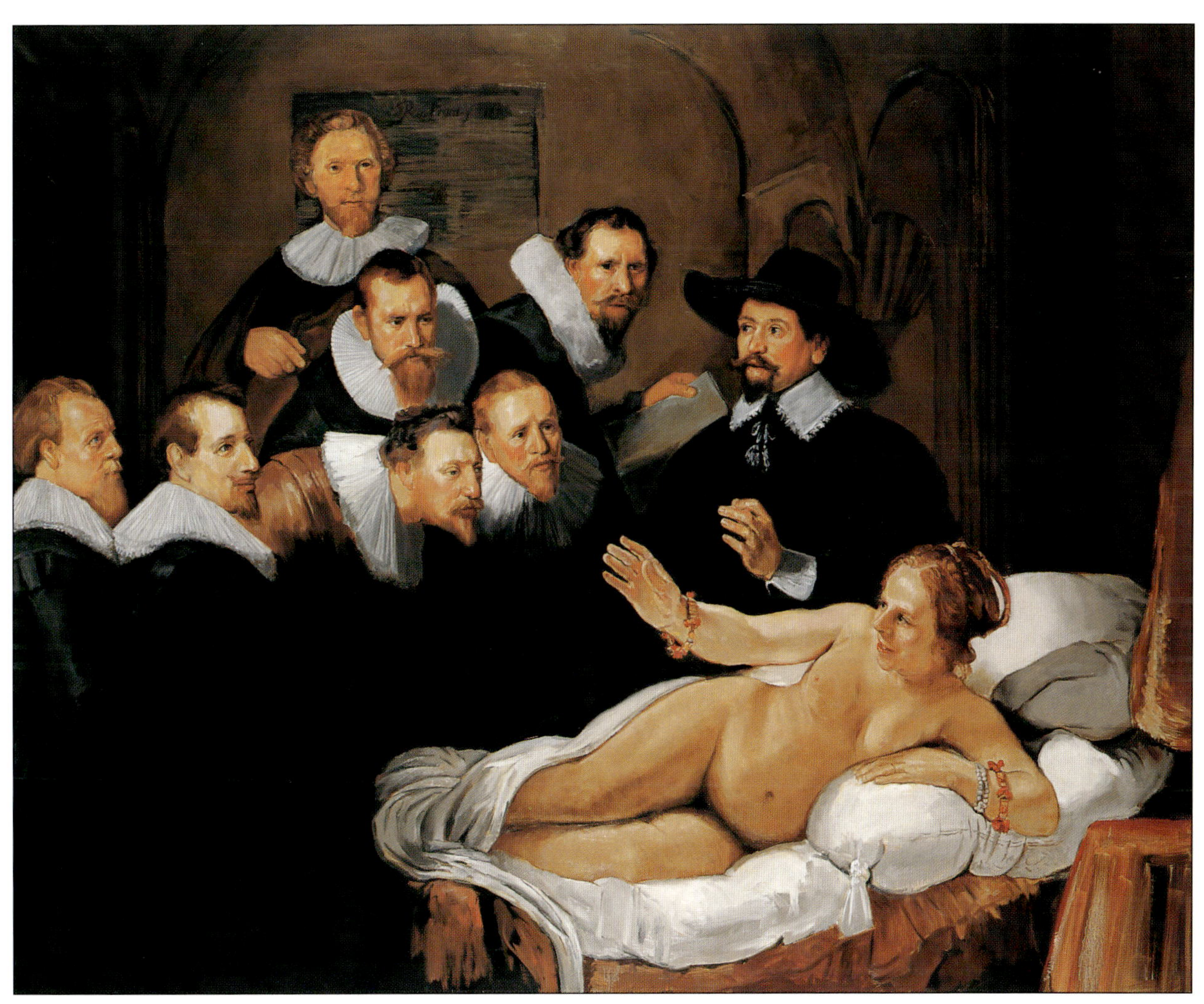

The Kidnapping of Modern Art by the New Yorkers

1985, 68 x 64 inches

Sources

Rubens, *The Abduction of the Daughters of Leucippus,* 1617, Alte Pinacotek, Munich

Picasso, *Les Demoiselles d'Avignon* (detail, adapted), 1907, Museum of Modern Art, New York

In the 1980s a French critic named Serge Guilbaut wrote a book called *How New York Stole the Idea of Modern Art*. Provoked by such works as Irving Sandler's famous *The Triumph of American Painting*, Guilbaut claimed that the postwar boom in the New York art world was due to a sinister conspiracy led by the U.S. government, with the aid of galleries and critics, to bring the center of the art world from Paris to New York. They did it by making Abstract Expressionism a symbol of artistic freedom and a weapon in the Cold War. I found this idea so appealing that I was inspired to call on my favorite Baroque painting, Rubens' *The Abduction of the Daughters of Leucippus*. To represent Modern Art, I replaced Rubens' weighty women (who couldn't have gotten on those horses with a forklift) with two figures I freely adapted from Picasso's revolutionary painting *Les Demoiselles d'Avignon*. The predatory men were originally intended to represent Castor and Pollux, the Gemini twins.

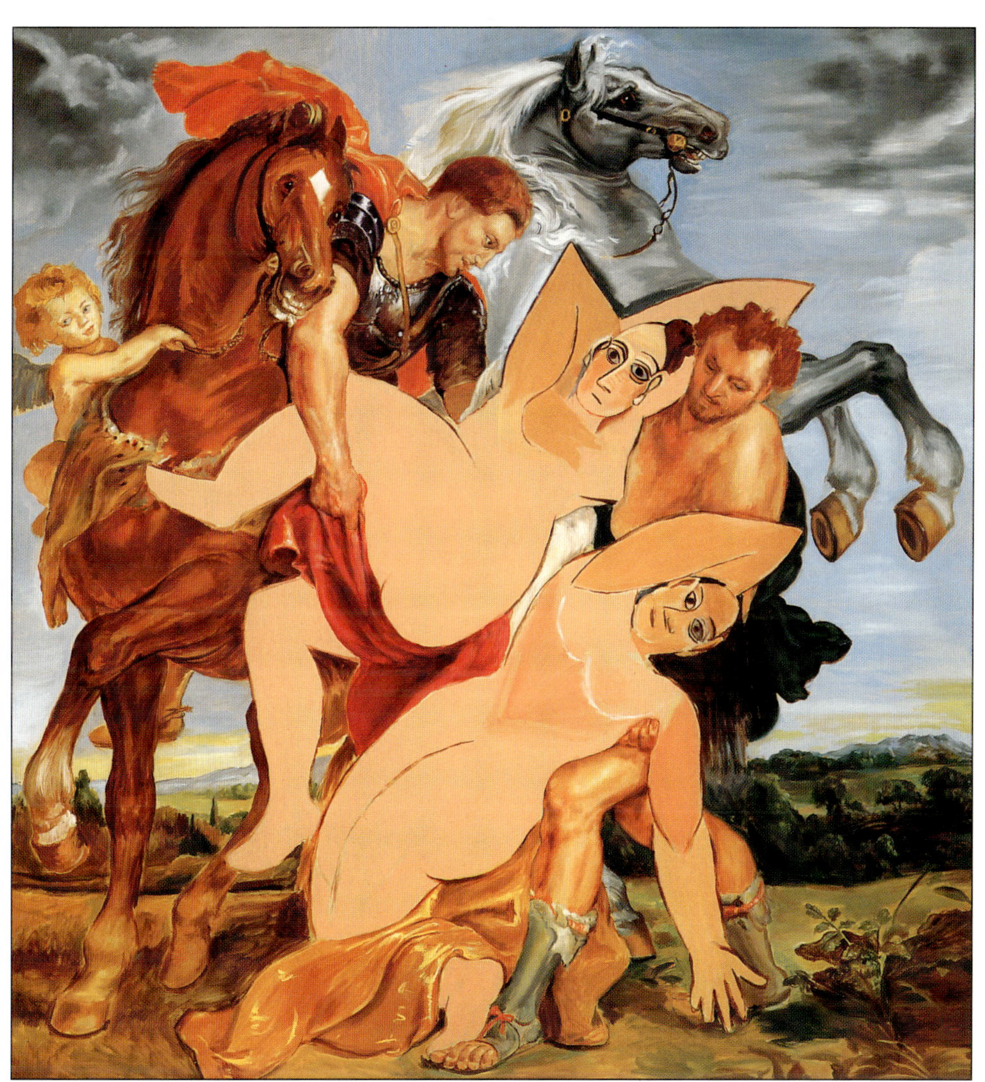

Overture to the Last Judgment

1985, 90 x 50 inches

Sources

Michelangelo, *The Last Judgment,* 1536–41, The Vatican, Rome

Degas, *Orchestra of the Paris Opéra,* 1868–69, Musée d'Orsay, Paris

Apparently I'm not the first to observe that the Christ figure in Michelangelo's *Last Judgment* in the Sistine Chapel seems to be conducting an orchestra. Leo Steinberg reported that the famous art historian Erwin Panofsky made the same observation in a London lecture in the forties. This distinguished pedigree does not, of course, excuse my eagerness to actually provide Him with musicians borrowed from Degas's tiny painting of the *Orchestra of the Paris Opéra*. One might think, with the millennium soon upon us, that they should pay more attention to the Conductor. Perhaps by then I will have finished this painting.

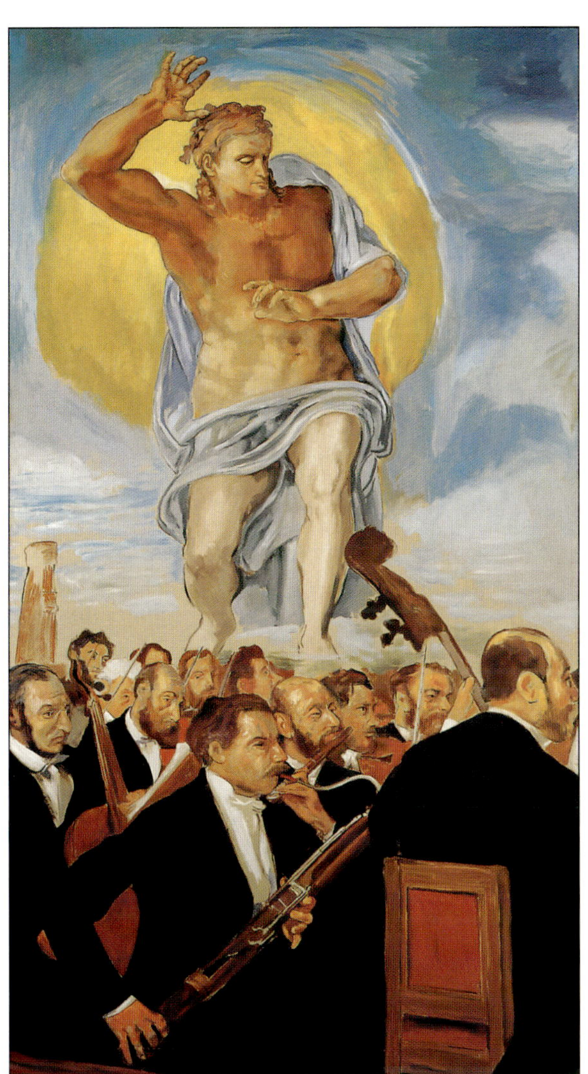

Sundance in Paris

1985, 48 x 60 inches

Sources

Caillebotte, *The Place de l'Europe on a Rainy Day,* 1877, Art Institute of Chicago

Renoir, *Dance at Bougival,* 1882–83, Museum of Fine Arts, Boston

Gustave Caillebotte's contribution to nineteenth-century French painting was twofold. Increasingly recognized as a talented painter whose promise was cut short by premature death, he is best known as a benefactor of his Impressionist friends. His generous bequest of their work to France is now one of the glories of the Musée d'Orsay. His generosity extended even to leaving a large open space in the lower left corner of one of his few acknowledged masterpieces, *The Place de l'Europe on a Rainy Day,* 1877. An amorous couple have waltzed in from a Renoir painting, so absorbed in each other that they have yet to realize the music is no longer playing, it's daylight, it's raining, and they're dancing on cobblestones. The respectable couple on the right now have something to look at, perhaps with nostalgia for their own distant, romantic younger selves.

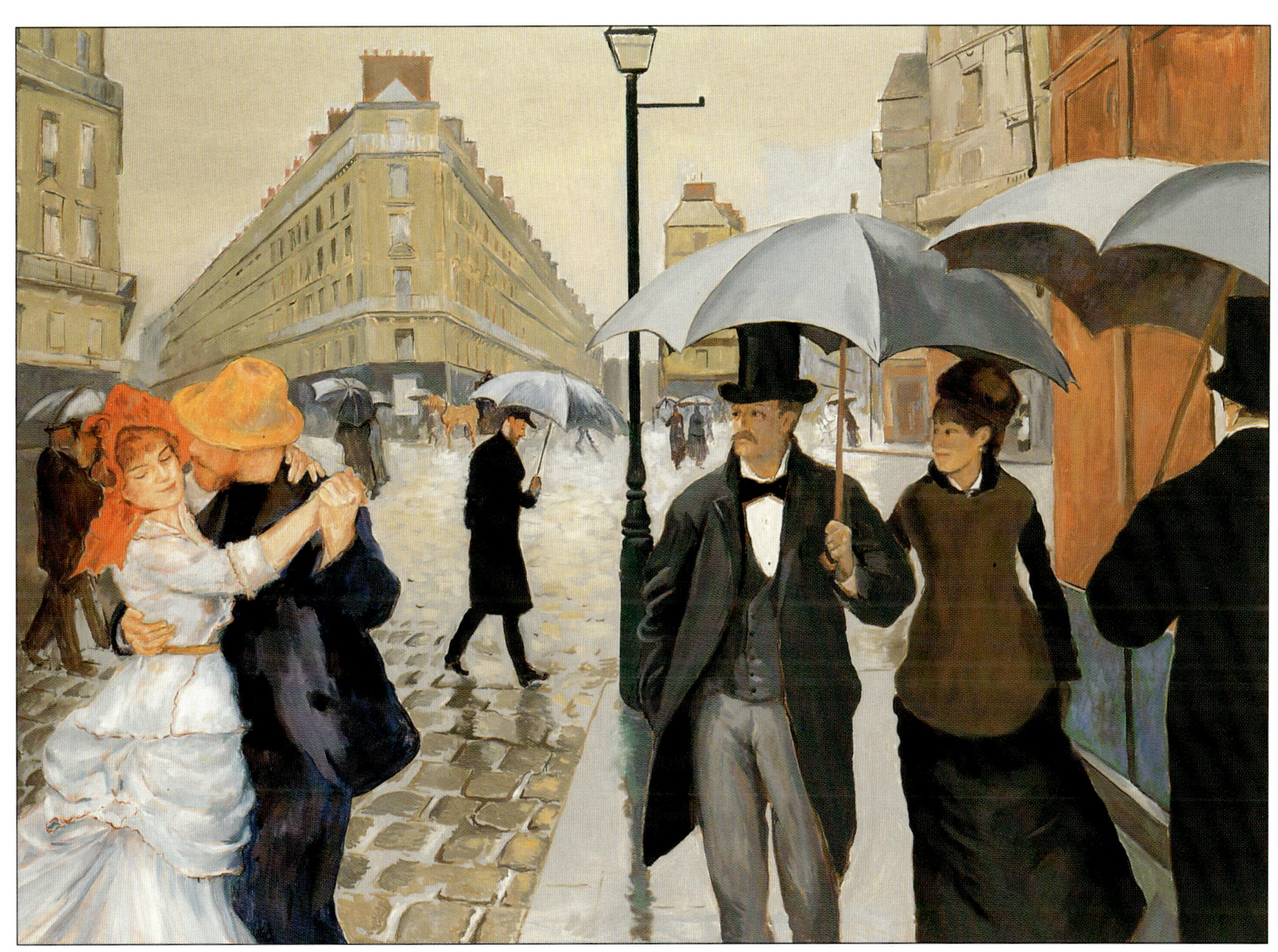

Dancing in the Rain

1986, 48 x 64 inches

Sources

Caillebotte, *The Place de l'Europe on a Rainy Day,* 1877, Art Institute of Chicago

Renoir, *Dance in the City,* 1882–83, Musée d'Orsay, Paris

When the *Sundance in Paris* was sold, it left a void in the studio that only fellow Paris sentimentalists will understand. I remembered that Renoir had painted more than *one* dancing couple. Although changing the dancers from out-of-towners to locals altered the composition, color, and mood somewhat and made it, to my mind, a new painting, I was concerned that the good friend who had acquired the "original" *Sundance* might be unhappy, so I showed him a photo of this work. He smiled amiably and said, "Burn it." What with one thing and another, I haven't gotten around to it yet.

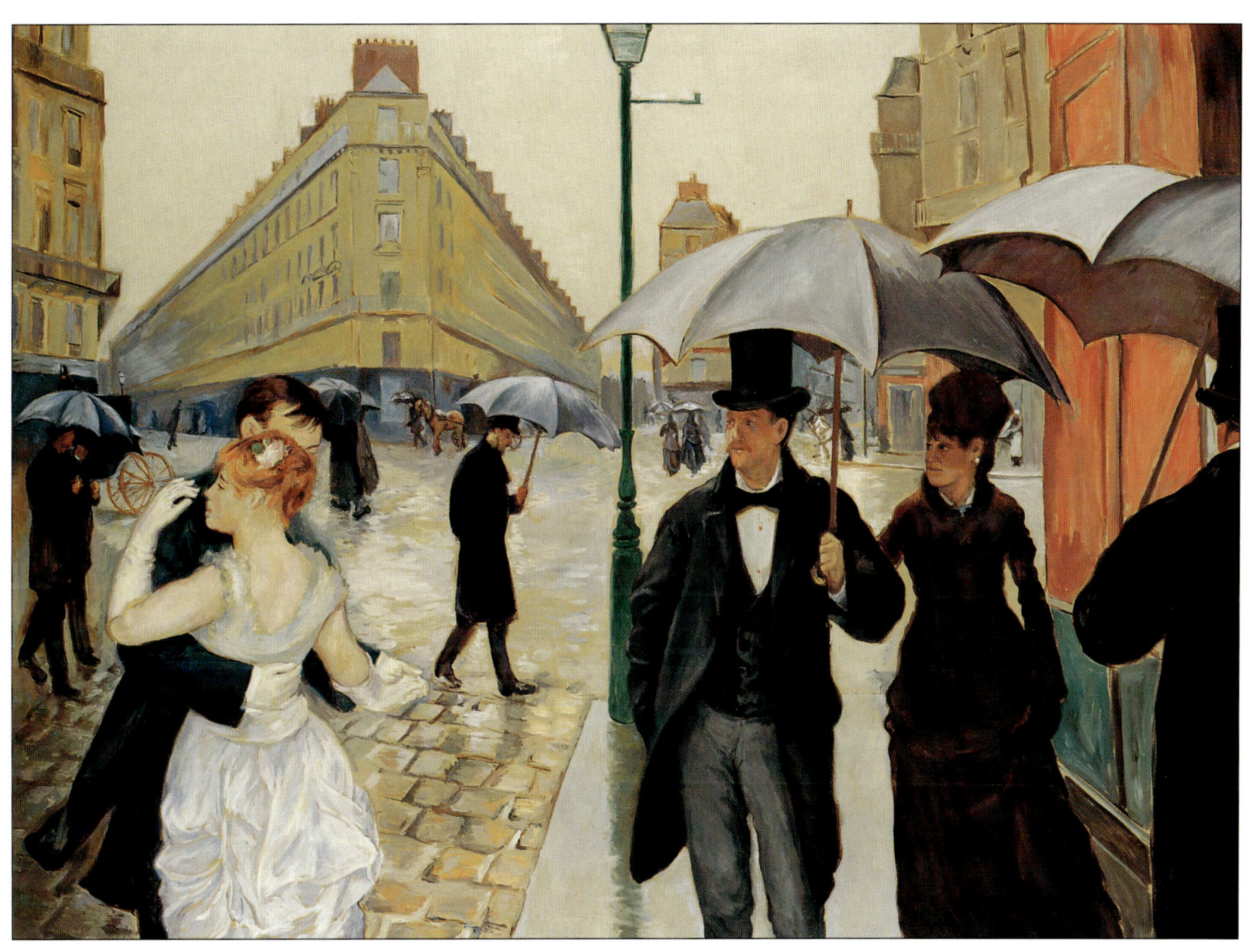

The Artist and His Family

1986, 60 x 48 inches

Sources

Courbet, *The Artist's Studio* (center detail), 1854–55, Musée d'Orsay, Paris

Courbet, *Woman with Parrot,* 1866, Metropolitan Museum of Art, New York

One admires some artists for their depth or their composition, others for their color or their brushwork. I always admired Gustave Courbet for his *ego*. Writing a book about one's life and work is one thing, but it takes a monumental self-regard to paint a large painting with oneself in the middle, surrounded by admirers from different places and periods of your life. I took the center detail, showing the master at his easel with his model behind him. Aside from its rough, freehand sketchiness, the only change I made was to replace the rather dry landscape he was working on with a famous Courbet nude, the *Woman with Parrot*.

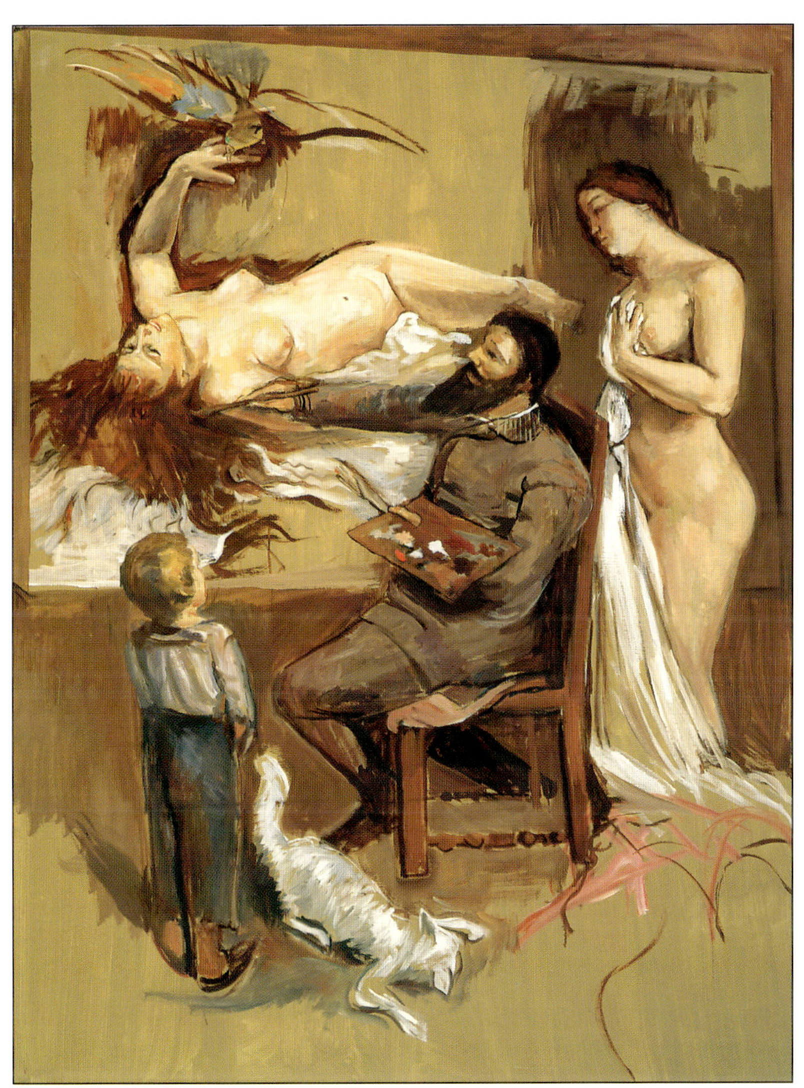

I Know You from Somewhere II

1986, 22 x 48 inches

Sources

Degas, *The Glass of Absinthe* (detail), 1876, Musée d'Orsay, Paris

Toulouse-Lautrec, *A La Mie,* 1891, Museum of Fine Arts, Boston

I thought these four should get to know one another. Toulouse-Lautrec was only twelve when Degas's *The Glass of Absinthe* (detail, couple on the left) was shown at the second Impressionist exhibition in Paris in 1876. Fifteen years later, he seemed to pay homage to his hero, Degas, with his own rather more disreputable couple. The characters are "played" by friends of the artists. The man at the right was the Paris representative of Moët and Chandon champagne.

The first version of my painting had its own neighboring table story. As I showed a photo of it to a friend in a bistro in Trouville, a stranger at the next table leaned over and offered to buy it. I brought it over from New York and delivered it personally. To this day, I don't know whether he liked the humor of it or just thought he was getting copies of a Degas and a Toulouse-Lautrec at a reasonable price. He and the painting then proceeded to do the greatest disappearing act since Houdini. Considering it lost forever, I decided to copy my own copy.

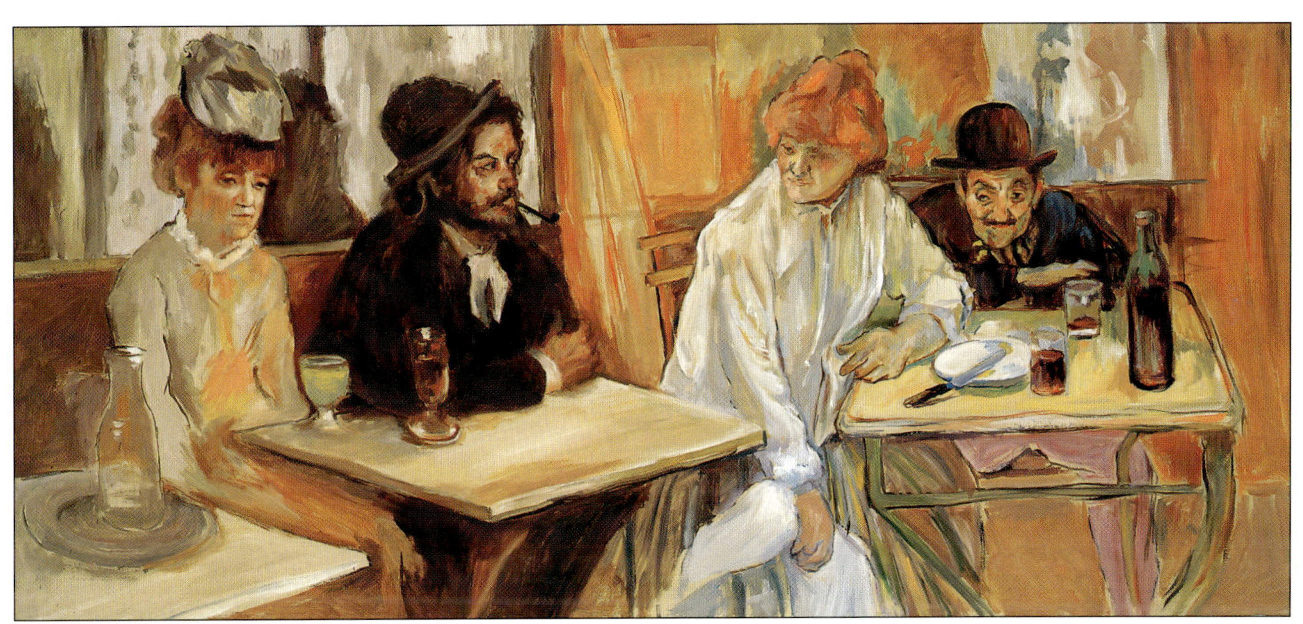

Love Conquers All

1986, 48 x 64 inches

Sources

Delacroix, *Dante and Virgil in Hell,* 1822, Louvre, Paris

Courbet, *Sleep,* 1866, Museum of the Petit-Palais, Paris

Eugène Delacroix achieved celebrity at the age of twenty-four with his *The Barque of Dante*, sometimes known as *Dante and Virgil in Hell.* It showed his debt to Rubens and Michelangelo and his friend Géricault, and it established his leadership of the French Romantics, alongside Victor Hugo and Hector Berlioz. Manet made a copy of it, now in the Metropolitan Museum. I have admired it since I first saw it in an art book in the forties, but it is a little depressing. I added two souls, who seem not to be tormented, from a painting entitled *Sleep* by the Realist Courbet.

In 1986, John Paoletti wrote in *Arts* magazine, "In *Love Conquers All,* the female as object of the male gaze remains voluptuous and tantalizing in the form of Courbet's two female lovers in the lower left corner. And yet the men in the painting, while hardly being able to deny their voyeuristic fascination, lift their hands as if in a gesture of horror or damnation, giving us a powerful representation of the old double standard in this double image."

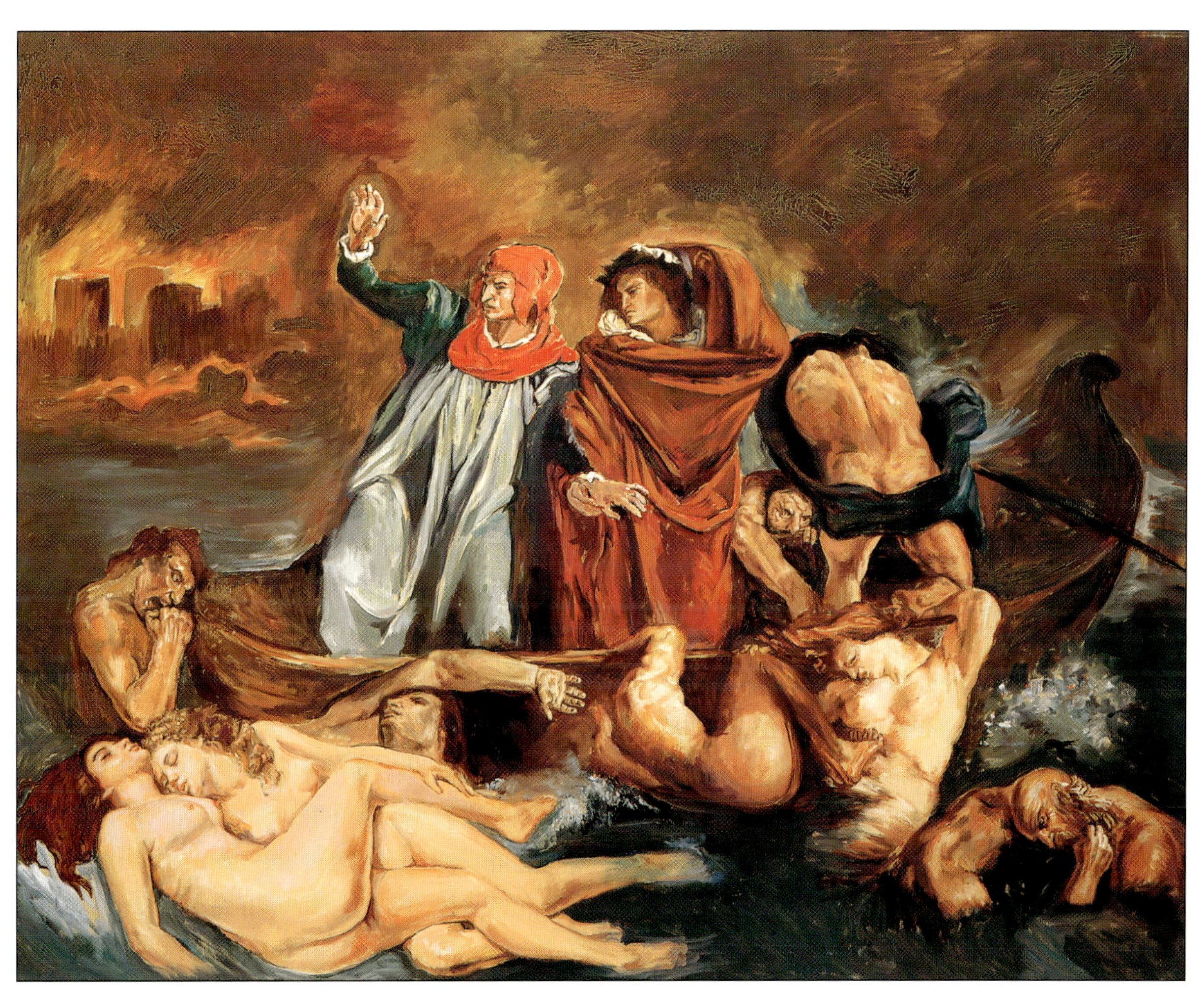

The Eve of St. Vincent

1986, 36 x 48 inches

Sources

Van Gogh, *Self-Portrait,* 1890, Musée d'Orsay, Paris

Van Gogh, *Starry Night,* 1889, Museum of Modern Art, New York

Attempting to reproduce the intensity of Van Gogh is a doomed enterprise, but I was curious to see what he might look like standing in the midst of one of his landscapes. The original self-portrait, painted after his breakdown in Arles, is one of his last, and one of the greatest.

Both this portrait and the imaginary night scene were executed while he was a patient at Saint-Rémy. Ironically, it was a time when his work was beginning to be recognized in Paris and Brussels, inspiring such passion among his friends that Toulouse-Lautrec challenged a mediocre artist to a duel for maligning him. Van Gogh copied often from artists he admired, especially Millet, but he called them "translations," adapting them freely into his own vision.

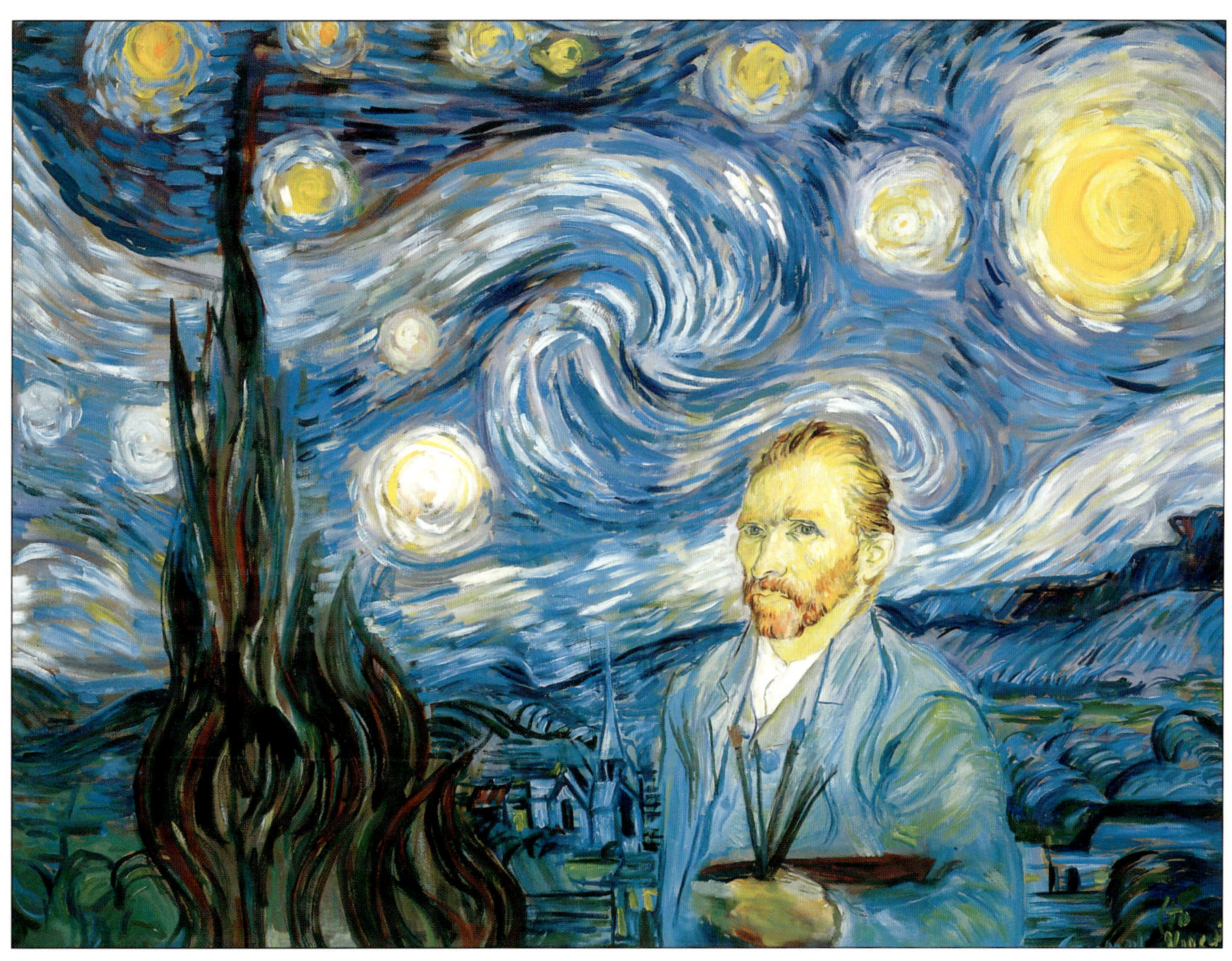

Déjeuner à la Carte

1986, 18 x 22 inches

Sources

Manet, *Luncheon on the Grass* (detail), 1863, Musée d'Orsay, Paris

Cézanne, *The Card Players* (detail), 1890, Musée d'Orsay, Paris

She has such a great poker face, it's surprising she's doing so poorly. It is the same air of imperturbable frankness with which she first stared down shocked Parisians from Manet's scandalous masterpiece, *Luncheon on the Grass*. This painting seems so flagrantly sexist that I hasten to quote again the art historian John Paoletti, who ascribed to me a more lofty motive: "Connor is concerned with how women have been represented in art history." It's hardly a secret that women have been treated badly as artists and as models. Manet, I think, should get credit for recognizing and revealing, in her confrontational gaze, the intelligent self-awareness of his favorite model. Victorine Meurent herself became a painter of some note, once having a work accepted in a Salon that rejected Manet's entry.

Cézanne's *Card Players* was one of five variations on that theme. Stolen in 1961, the painting was recovered soon after the French government publicized it on a postage stamp.

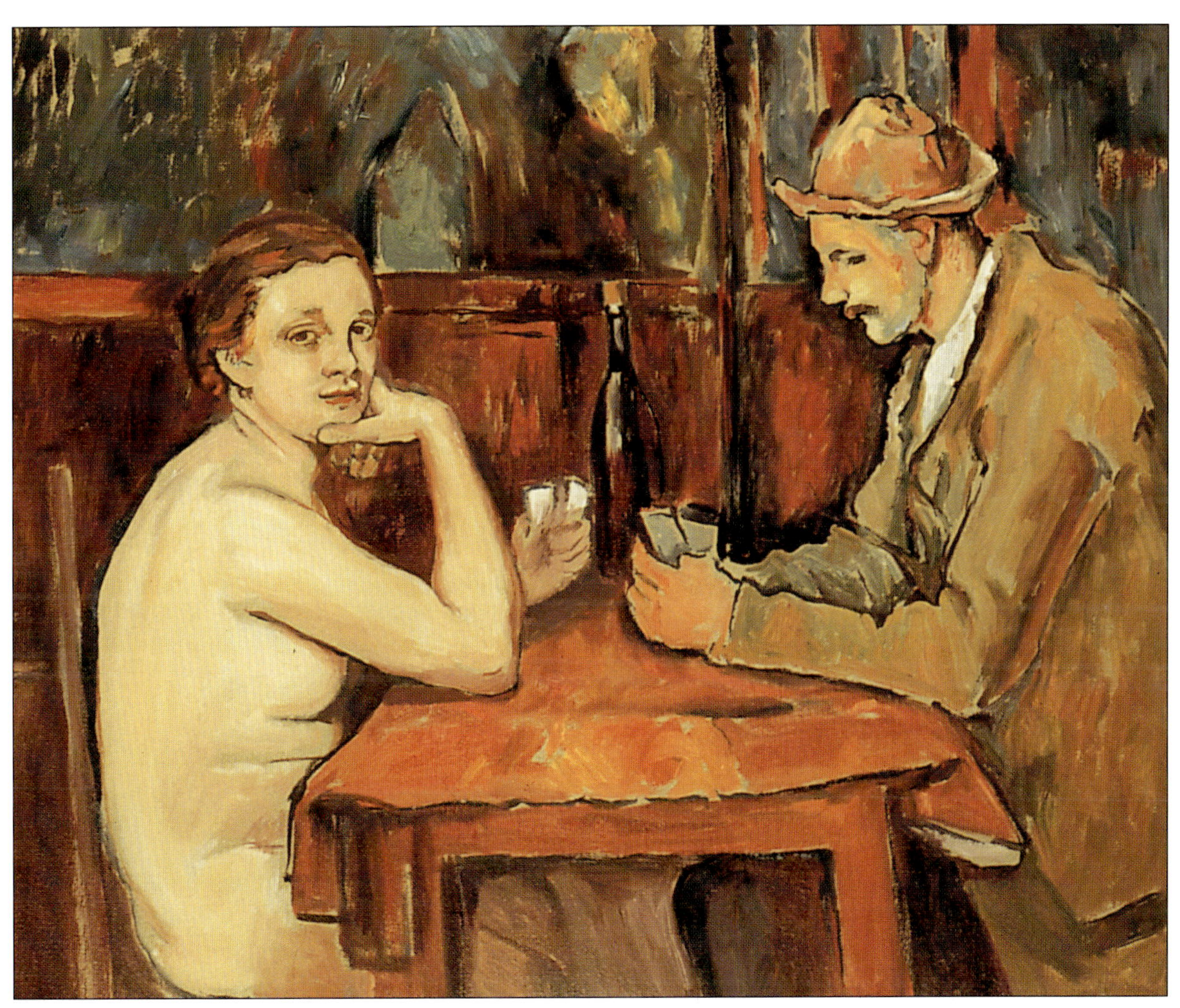

Strangers on a Train

1986, 30 x 40 inches

Sources

Daumier, *The Third-Class Carriage,* 1864, Metropolitan Museum of Art, New York

Daumier, *Scapin and Silvester,* 1864, Musée d'Orsay, Paris

Daumier painted all three classes of train passengers, but it was *The Third-Class Carriage* that brought out his greatest qualities, matching a Michelangelesque power of drawing to his deep fund of human empathy. The serenity, however, may be temporary, as passengers in the rear have been replaced by two figures from another Daumier painting, *Scapin and Silvester,* characters from Molière who are clearly up to no good.

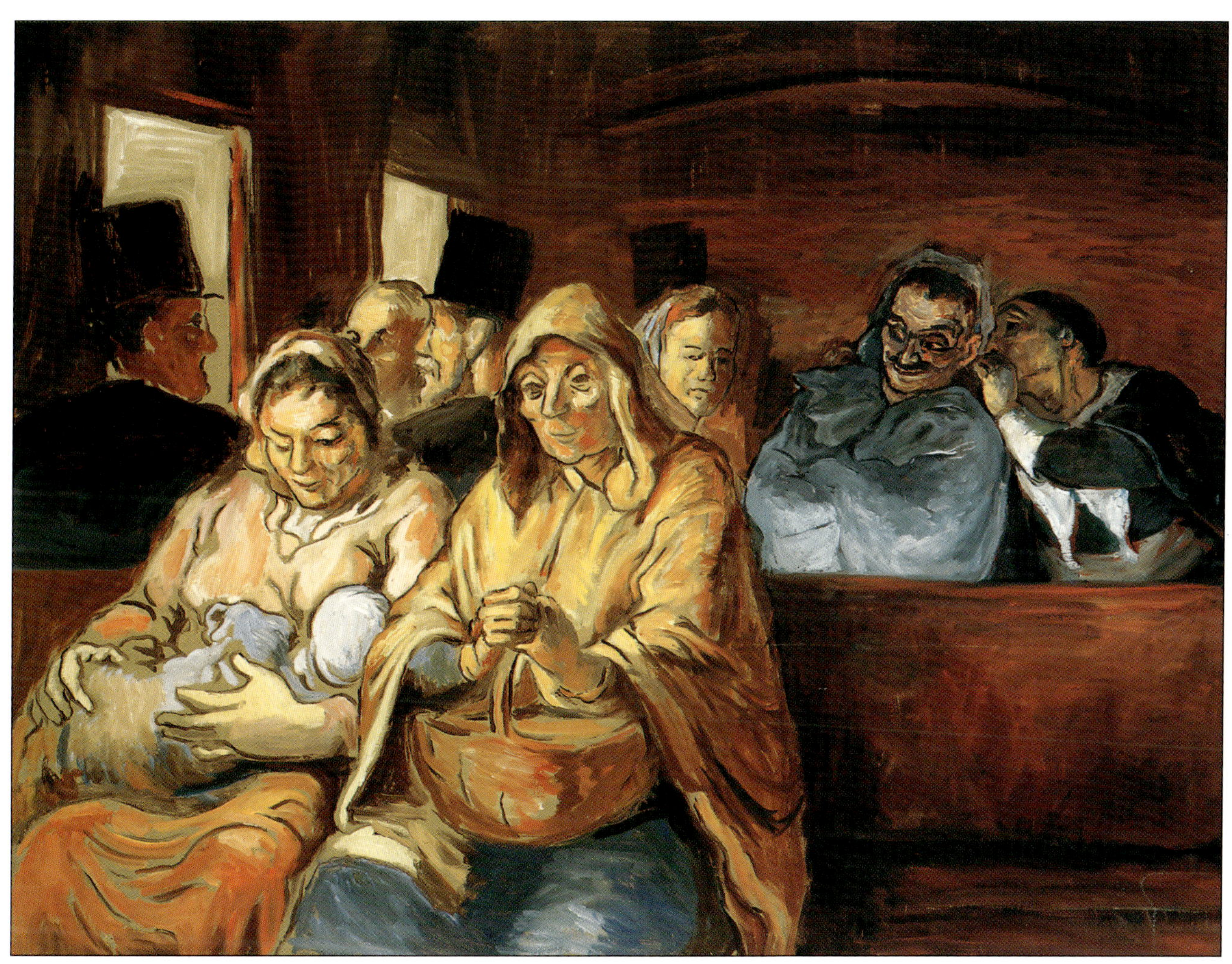

The Discovery of Venus

1986, 35 x 52 inches

Sources

Géricault, *The Raft of the Medusa* (detail), 1818, Louvre, Paris

Cabanel, *The Birth of Venus*, 1863, Musée d'Orsay, Paris

The desperate survivors in Géricault's huge, fact-based *Raft of the Medusa* were originally waving to the distant gunboat that rescued them. On July 2, 1816, a French frigate carrying soldiers and settlers to the colony of Senegal was wrecked on a reef off the African coast. It became a major scandal because of the incompetence and cowardice of the "aristocratic" captain: only fifteen survived of the hundred and fifty he had abandoned on a jerry-built raft to face thirteen days of insanity, mutiny, and cannibalism. The painting, which did much to undermine the Davidian tradition of glorifying human will and heroic action, was a great success when displayed to a ticket-buying public in London and Dublin.

Who knows what fantasies filled the horizon until the moment of rescue? The ultimate barroom nude, by Cabanel, presents itself as one possibility.

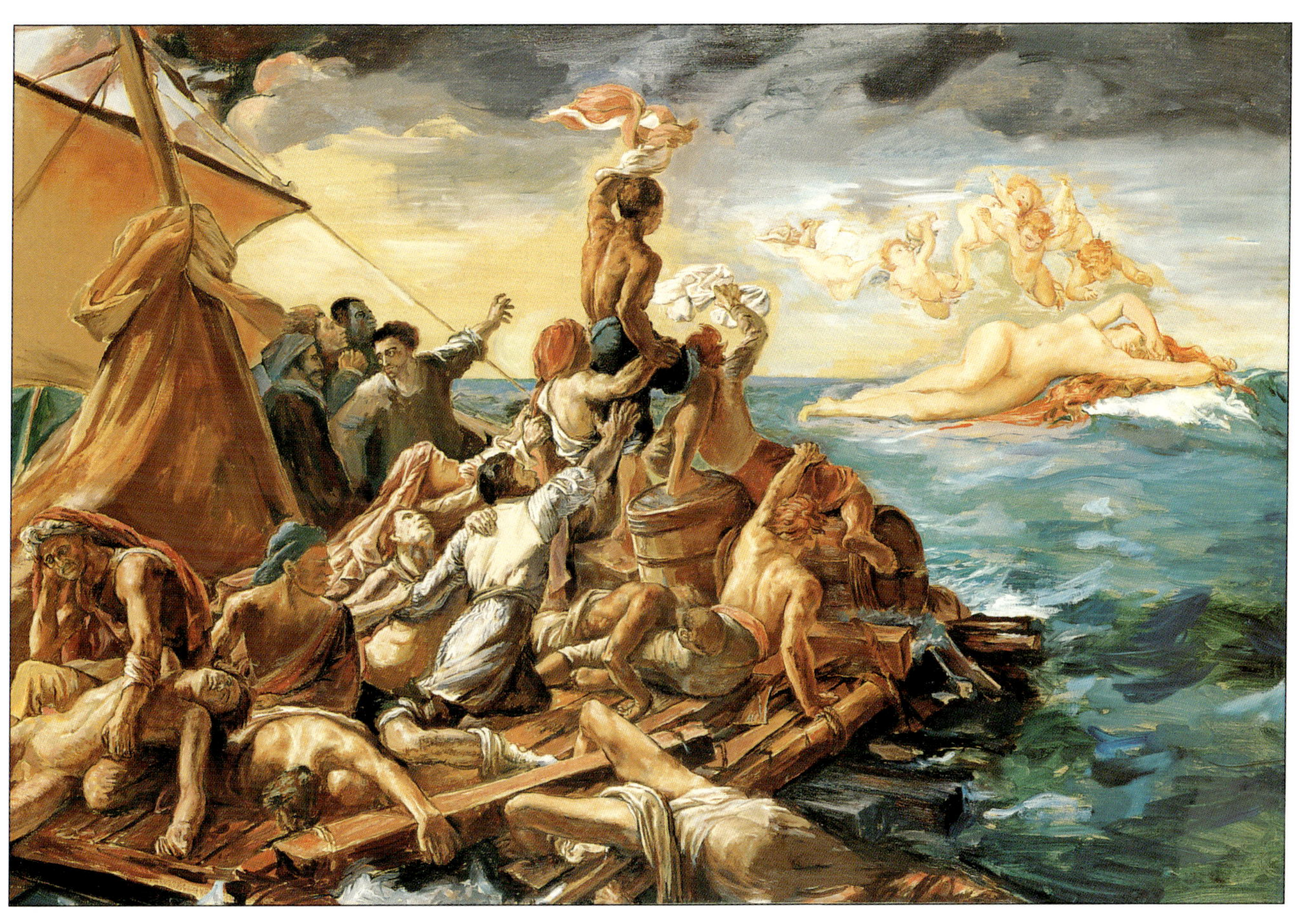

God Helps Those . . .

1986, 33 x 33 inches

Sources

Millet, *The Angelus,* 1858, Musée d'Orsay, Paris

Millet, *The Gleaners,* 1857, Musée d'Orsay, Paris

One must be of a certain age and, perhaps, have been educated in a Catholic school to realize how ubiquitous reproductions of Jean François Millet's *The Angelus* were at one time. Inspired by the church bells that remind the devout to pray at daybreak, noon, and day's end, it was treated as an admirable example of religious fervor among the pure of heart, with no talk of art or social conditions or the widespread famine. Even further down the social ladder than the farm workers were *The Gleaners*, permitted to scavenge for leavings after the crop had been harvested and too busy to hear for whom the bells toll.

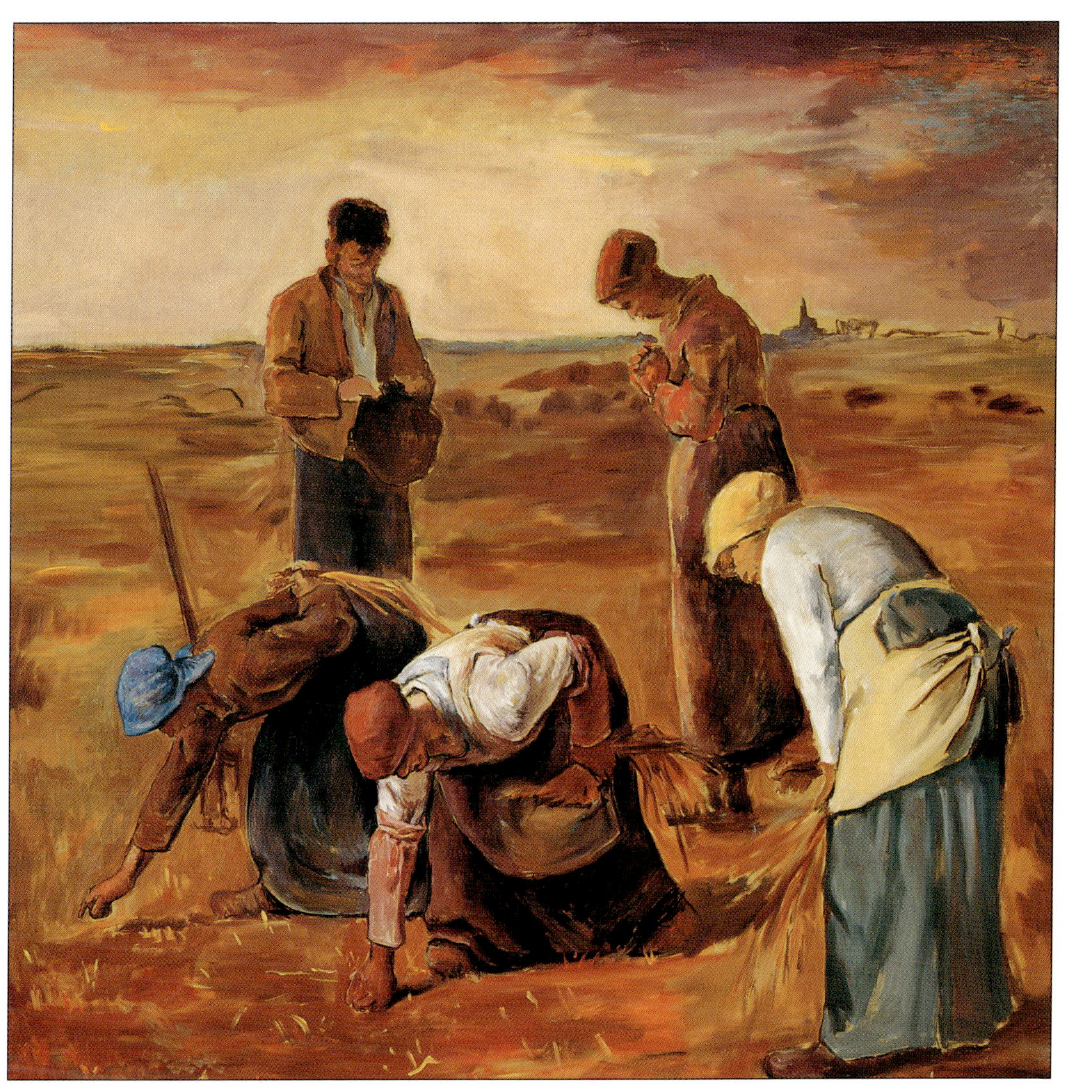

The Spanish Visitors

1986, 66 x 50 inches

Sources

Manet, *The Balcony,* 1868–69, Musée d'Orsay, Paris

Goya, *Majas on a Balcony* (workshop version?), 1811, Metropolitan Museum of Art, New York

This painting relates to *I Know You from Somewhere II* (page 41). Both works join a painting to an earlier one that appears to have been its inspiration. In this case, they are the two most famous balcony scenes since Romeo and Juliet. Goya's *Majas on a Balcony,* with two women of uncertain virtue leaning on a railing and two mysterious men lurking behind, must have hovered in Manet's imagination when he painted his own *The Balcony* almost sixty years later. Both paintings haunted me, so I replaced three background figures in Manet's painting with three fugitives from Goya's work, who now join Manet's friend and sister-in-law, the artist Berthe Morisot, prominent in the left foreground. This painting represents for me the way that artists, to varying degrees, contend with, or live happily with, the phantoms of their great predecessors. For the further adventures of Goya's *Majas on a Balcony* see page 88.

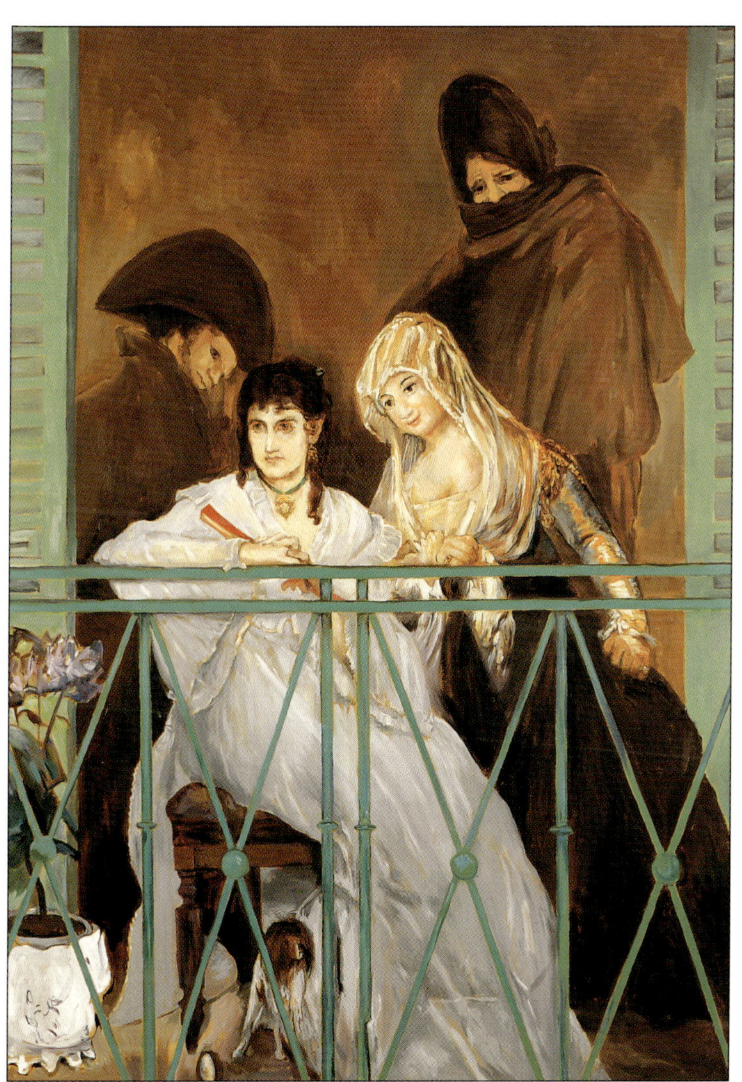

Royal Wedding

1986, 68 x 50 inches

Sources

Gainsborough, *The Blue Boy,* 1770, Huntington Library, Pasadena

Lawrence, *Pinkie,* 1795, Huntington Library, Pasadena

They have been together a long time, in the same collection, in books and slides, and in the imagination. In darkened classrooms, art history professors are likely to show them side by side. I simply pushed them a little closer. Sarah Moulton-Barrett, known as Pinkie, was only twelve when her portrait was painted, and died tragically a year later. My version doesn't yet do justice to her radiant youth and charm or to the artist, Thomas Lawrence; let's call it a copy in progress. Apparently what I aspired to do here was to perform a spiritual marriage, across time and space. The popular story that Gainsborough painted Jonathan Buttall in blue to challenge Joshua Reynolds's assertion that a great portrait could not be dominantly blue was invented after Gainsborough's death and after Reynolds himself had painted many fine portraits in blue.

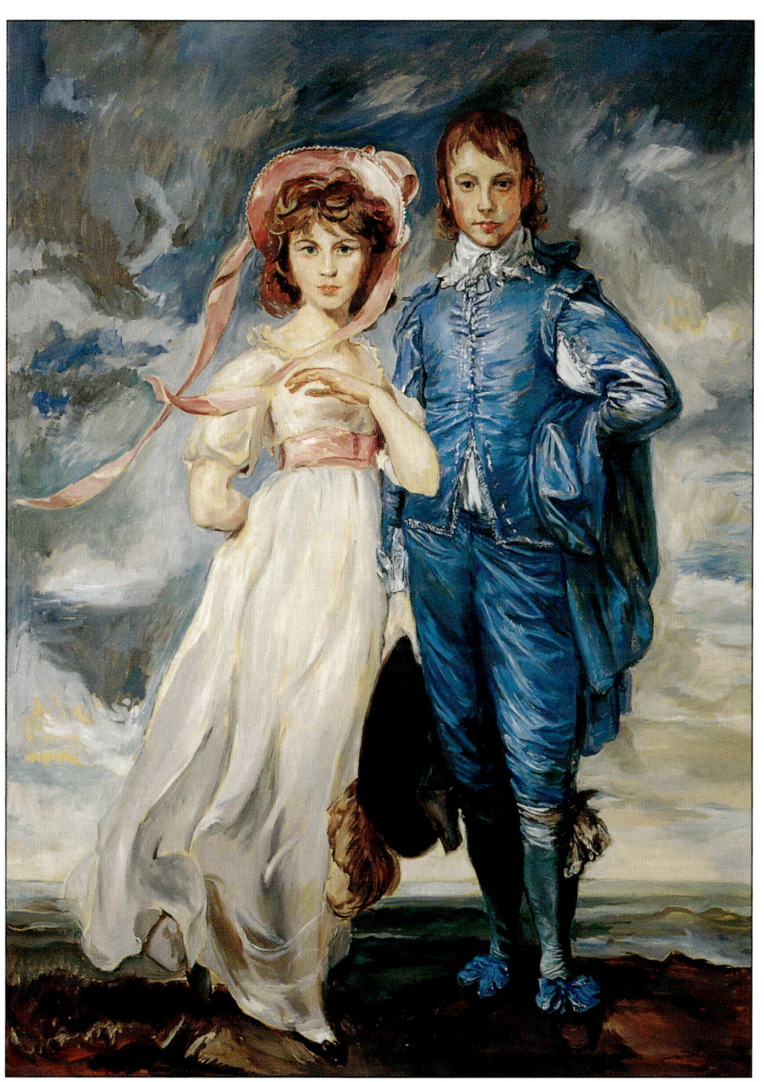

Club Tahiti

1987, 48 x 60 inches

Sources

Renoir, *Luncheon of the Boating Party,* 1881, Phillips Collection, Washington, D.C.

Gauguin, *Tahitian Women with Mango Blossoms,* 1899, Metropolitan Museum of Art, New York

This is my anti-colonialist painting. Renoir painted the affluent young bohemians and bourgeoisie of his time as they wished to see themselves in his famous *Luncheon of the Boating Party*. His friend and benefactor, the painter Caillebotte, smoking, leans on the back of a chair at the right. Renoir's future wife sits at the left, playing with a little dog. Charming as it seems, it was the sort of society that Gauguin tried to put behind him when he left France, looking to find in Tahiti a purer, more innocently savage state of nature (hoping, also, that paintings of that world might sell as well in Paris as the exotic tales of Pierre Loti). He arrived late. The French colonial authorities and missionaries had already been happily about their work of repressing, converting, and covering up bodies, a process Gauguin did his best to reverse. By joining the two worlds, my painting represents the familiar phenomenon of older, or less "civilized," cultures seeking to survive by displaying their picturesqueness to the tourists. Now, of course, it's the Tahitians who would look most at home on the beach at St. Tropez.

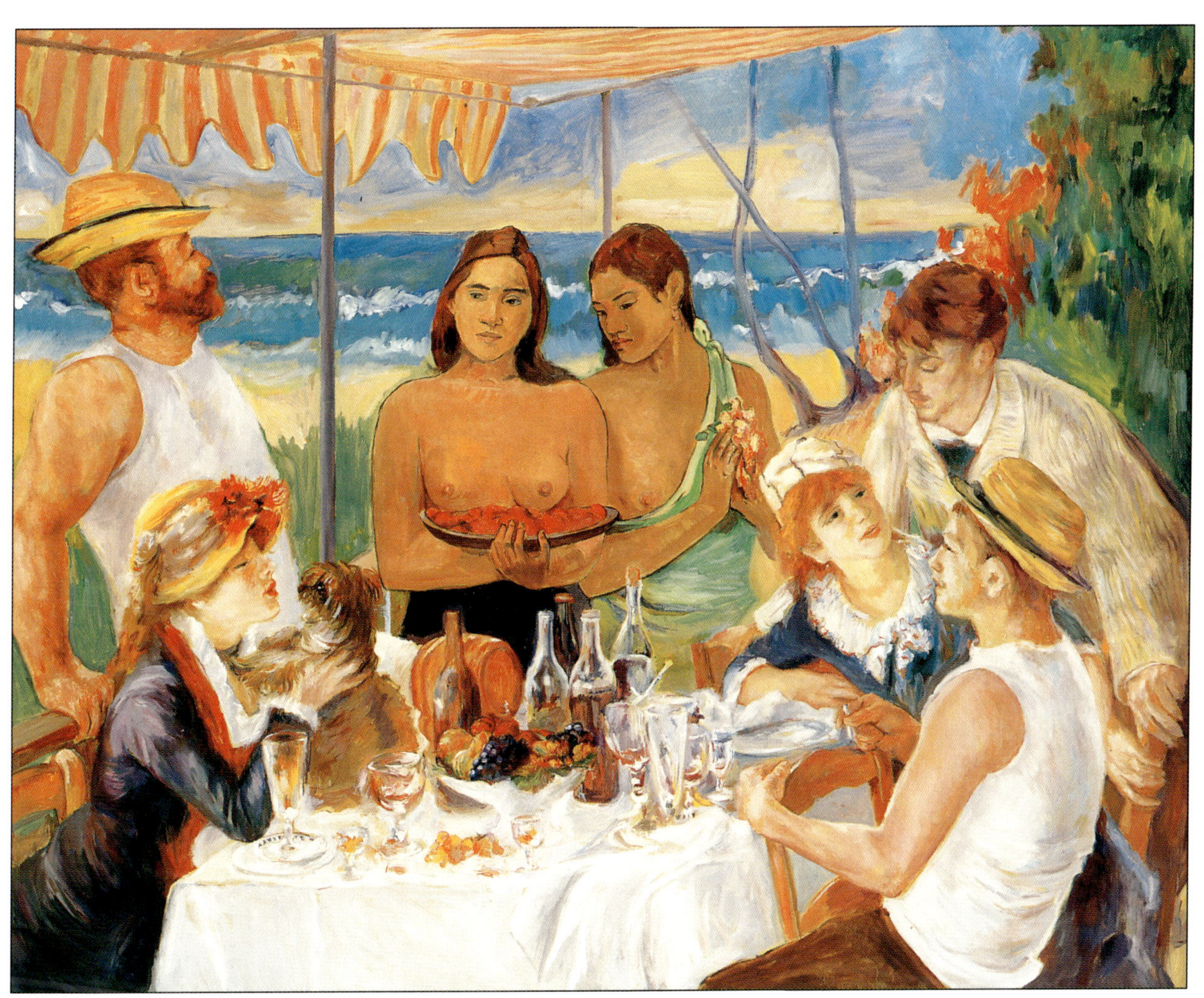

The Prints of Zola

1996, 48 x 60 inches

Source

Manet, *Portrait of Emile Zola,* 1868, Musée d'Orsay, Paris

Dreyfus was not the first unjustly accused victim defended by Emile Zola. Edouard Manet's paintings were under ferocious attack by conservative critics, and Zola sprang to his support: "It is impossible that Manet will not have his day of triumph and . . . obliterate the timid mediocrities who surround him." The small painting within a painting suggests what the original work looks like, surrounded here by the sort of play with scale familiar to us from the graphics of modern print and TV advertising. Manet's portrait of his friend pays tribute to his own artistic sources. Zola holds in his lap an illustrated history of European art, while behind him the influence of Spanish painting, represented by Goya's engraving of Velasquez' *Feast of Bacchus,* and Japanese woodblock prints (a Sumo wrestler by Kuniaki) are juxtaposed with a print of his own *Olympia,* which had been eloquently defended by Zola. It was the first recognition in a major painting of the impact of the growing art reproduction industry on a modern sensibility and was thus, for me, a direct ancestor of the work in this book.

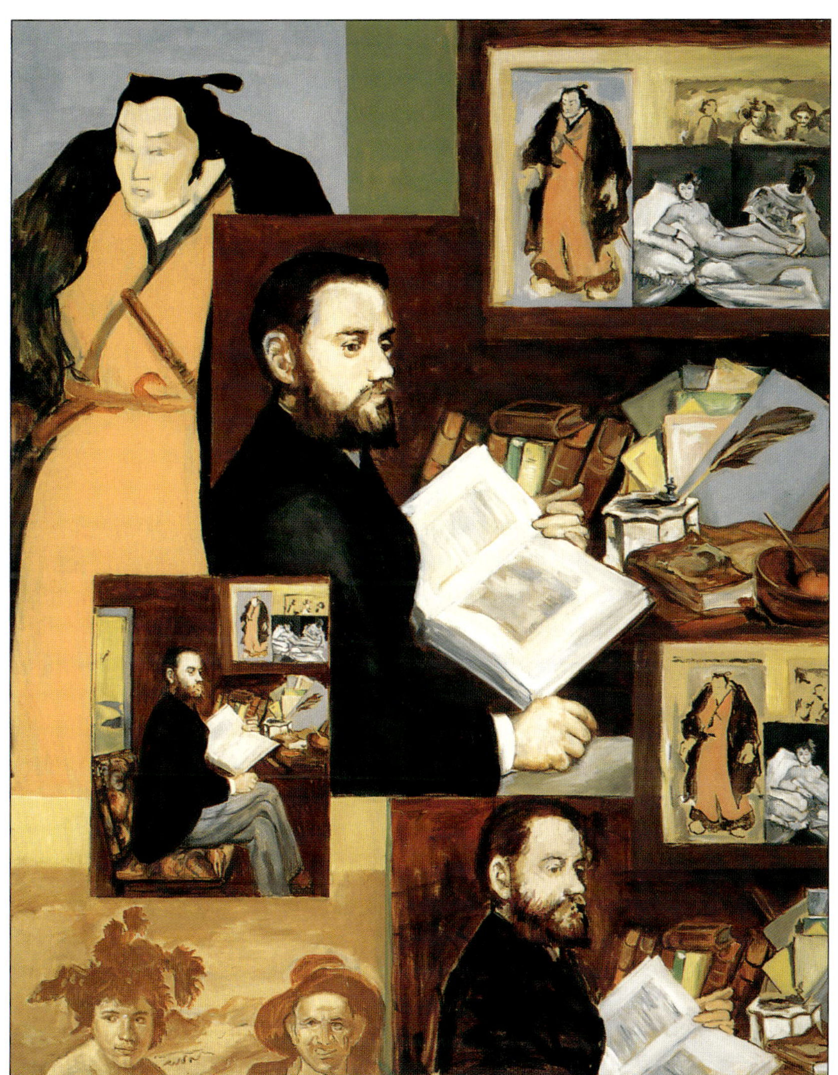

The Opening I

1988, 48 x 64 inches

Sources

Manet, *Luncheon on the Grass,* 1863, Musée d'Orsay, Paris

Manet, *A Bar at the Folies-Bergère,* 1881, Courtauld Institute, London

In the original painting, Manet's perplexing last masterpiece, *A Bar at the Folies-Bergère,* the barmaid, Suzon, stood in front of a large mirror that reflected a chandelier, a smoky, crowded balcony, the bottles on the bar, and a view of her back at an odd angle as she talks to a customer who is mysteriously not present in the foreground. She always looked to me as though she were serving at an exhibition opening, so I rescued her from this confusion and transported her to a museum. It turns out to be a Manet show, and now she welcomes guests in front of his first masterpiece, *Luncheon on the Grass,* in which Victorine Meurent plays the leading role. Even Manet would agree that my painting is less ambiguous than his, although I'm not sure he would appreciate the tidy fashion in which I have summed up his career. Suzon posed for Manet in his studio, and a lot of ink and paper have been expended in interpreting her social significance and questioning her morals. In *The Painting of Modern Life,* T. J. Clarke wrote: "She does not seem . . . to be firmly part of the bourgeoisie; and that is the key to her modernity. . . . The look is a special one: public, outward, blasé, impassive, not bored, not tired, not disdainful, not quite focused on anything."

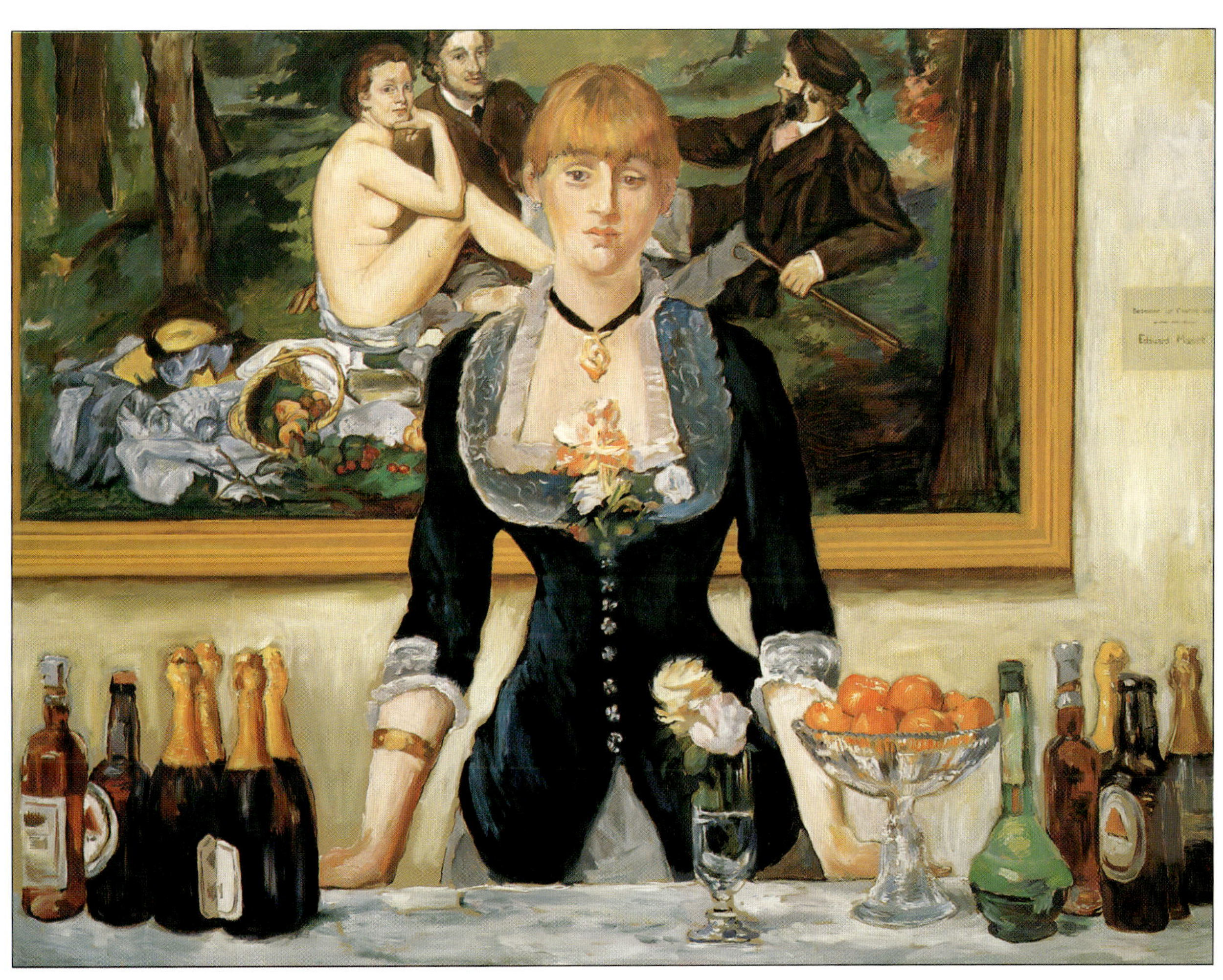

The Opening II

1990, 48 x 60 inches

Source

Manet, *A Bar at the Folies-Bergère,* 1881, Courtauld Institute, London

The departure of *The Opening* to a happy home in the Clark collection left a large void in the studio. Well, I thought, in a museum, if a painting is shipped out, you hang something else in its place. If I put a different work behind the barmaid, wouldn't I be creating a new painting? Here she is standing in front of Manet's last masterpiece, in which she herself is posed in front of a mirror while her oddly off-center reflection leans over to serve a mysterious customer. This time, placing a puzzle inside an enigma, I've managed to make a painting that is *more* ambiguous than Manet's. She is, in fact, doubly beside herself—and so would you be if you didn't know from one day to the next what painting would be your home.

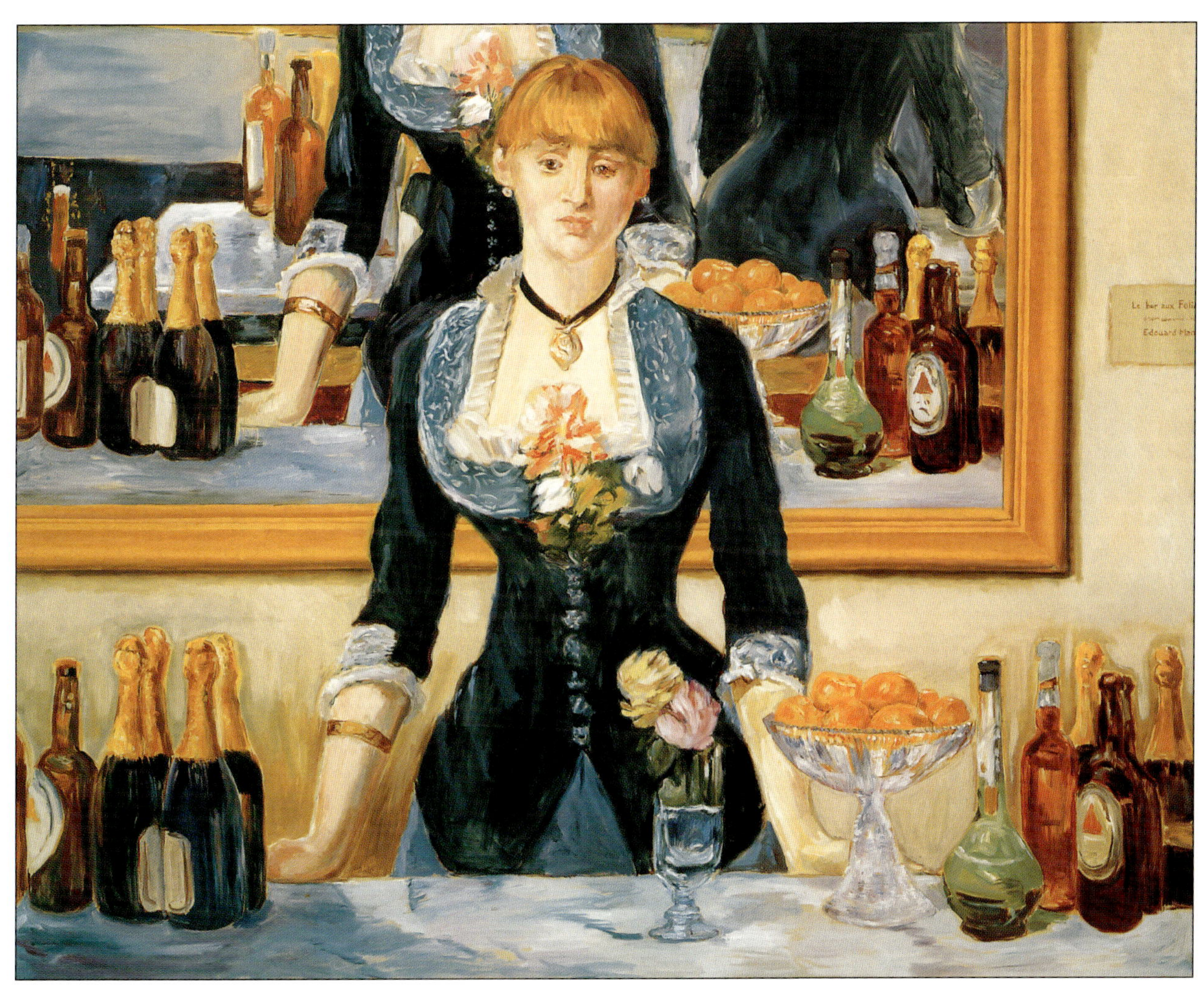
Le bar aux
Edouard

Arranging the Model

1988, 36 x 46 inches

Sources

Manet, *Gare Saint-Lazare,* 1873,
National Gallery, Washington, D.C.

Manet, *In the Conservatory* (detail), 1879,
Staatliche Museen, Berlin

There are two intruders in this painting. As usual, I am the unseen one cheerfully disrupting the compositions of great artists, in this case ignoring the train station glimpsed through the bars and shattering the lovely, taut balance that bound the seated woman and the child. I've brought in another fellow, whose relation to them is not at all clear. Manet was breaking ground again; the original was the first *plein air* Impressionist painting shown in a Salon (1874). He had painted bold variations on the conventional Salon categories, such as history, religion, portraiture. Now he confronted the critics with a painting of real life with no obvious subject or anecdote, allying himself with the other Impressionists who already regarded him as their leader. The influence of Japanese woodcuts is clear in the sweeping curves played against the vertical pattern of the fence. The neutral situation of the seated woman and child encouraged viewers to make up their own stories, and so I did. I imagined Manet himself, acting like the director of a film or a photo shoot, stepping into the scene at the last minute to arrange the hair of the model, once again the indispensable Victorine Meurent. I found the artist's look-alike in another Manet painting in which he was originally holding a cigar in his left hand.

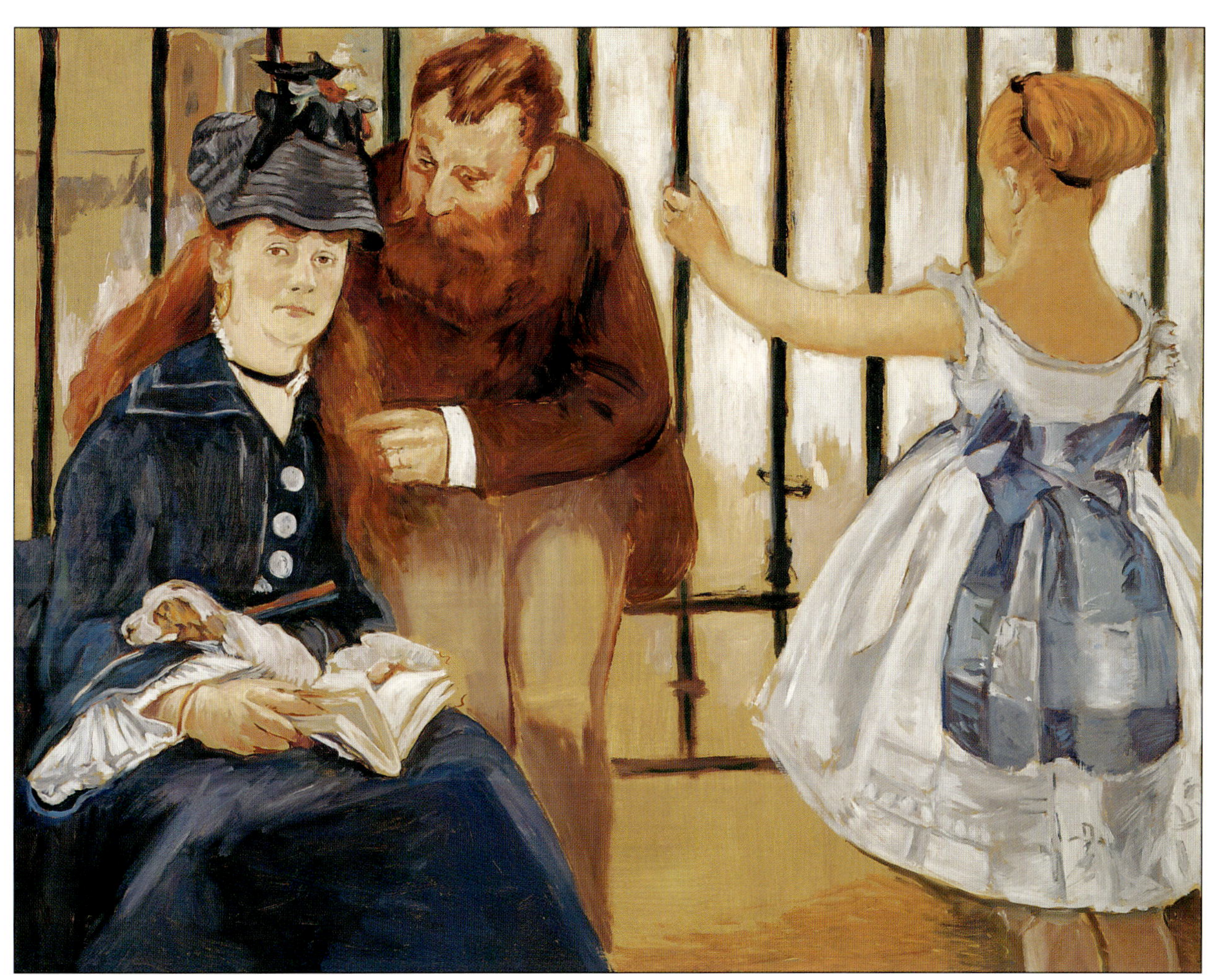

War and Peace

1989, 50 x 68 inches

Sources

Picasso, *Guernica,* 1937, Prado, Madrid

David, *The Oath of the Horatii,* 1784, Louvre, Paris

Botticelli, *Primavera,* 1477–78, Uffizi, Florence

Instead of putting two paintings together to make a new story, I wanted to try one of the classic themes, within which I could feel free to mix more far-ranging images. *War and Peace* seemed a properly grandiose subject. I didn't have any sharp or profound insights to offer on the world's penchant for disaster, so I thought of images that speak of folly, cruelty, and hope. The result is a sort of painted collage, with details from Picasso's *Guernica* hovering over fragments from David and Botticelli. It became a story of hands. Hands raised in a salute made forever sinister by Fascism, in David's *The Oath of the Horatii,* find a graceful challenge in the life-affirming gestures of Botticelli's three Graces from *Primavera*.

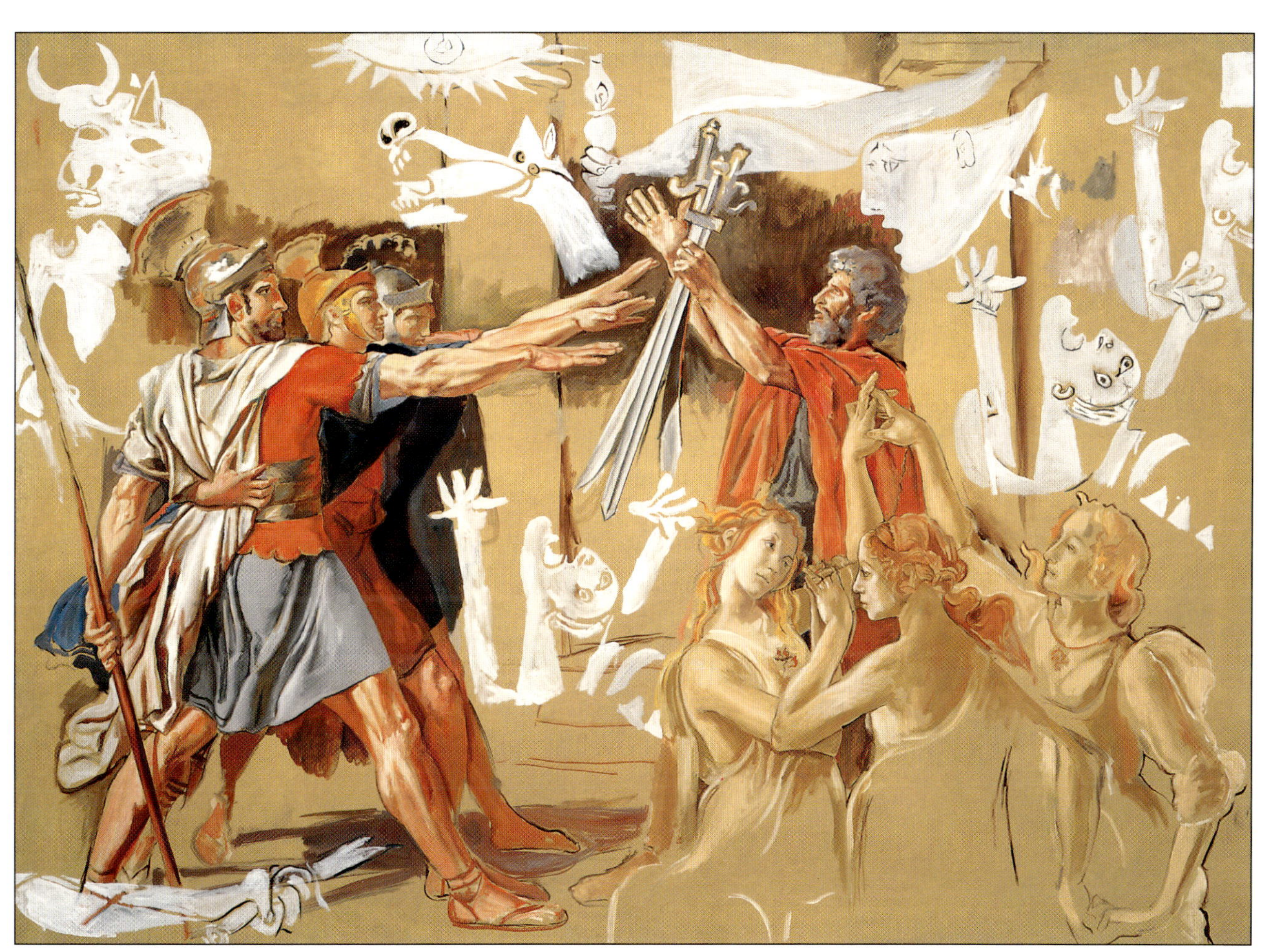

Save the NEA

1989, 48 x 76 inches

Sources

David, *The Sabine Women,* 1799, Louvre, Paris

Watteau, *Gilles,* 1717–19, Louvre, Paris

This was painted at the height of the controversy over government funding for the arts, especially grants for exhibitions of controversial artists like Robert Mapplethorpe and Andres Serrano. It's a complicated subject, and I'm not a great fan of their work, but the enemies they attracted made it clear which side I had to be on. Watteau's figure of *Gilles* in his cute little costume looked like someone who would have a rough time in the schoolyard, so I nominated him to represent the artists, and the brave woman who tried to stop the fighting in David's *The Sabine Women* could stand for those who defended them. I concluded that this work would have zero effect on NEA opponents (an ironic discrepancy is that the macho spear-thrower representing Helms/Armey/Gingrich showed up without his pants), and for everyone else it would be preaching to the converted, so this is its first public performance.

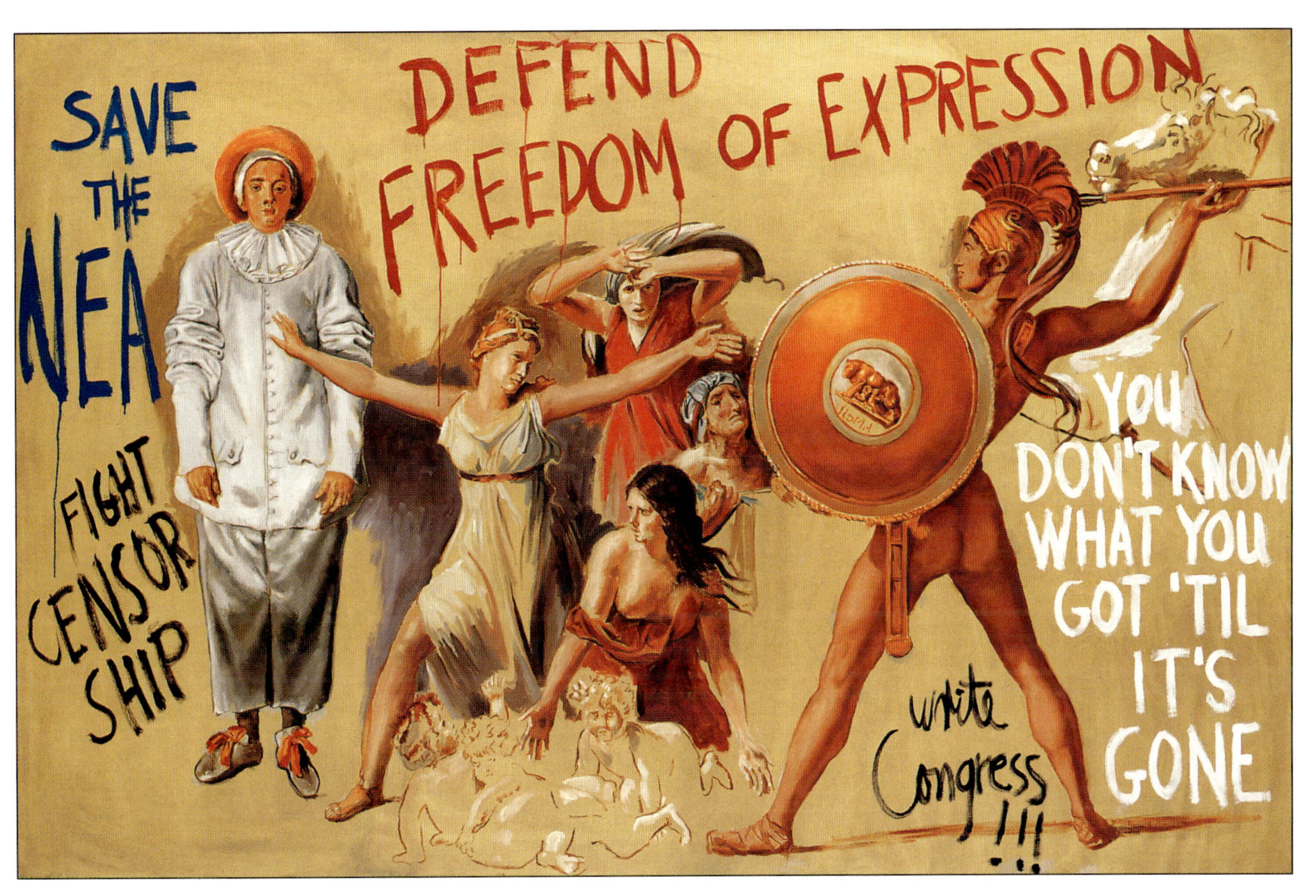
SAVE THE NEA
FIGHT CENSORSHIP
DEFEND FREEDOM OF EXPRESSION
YOU DON'T KNOW WHAT YOU GOT 'TIL IT'S GONE
write Congress !!!

Retirement

1989, 38 x 52 inches

Sources

Monet, *Terrace at Sainte-Adresse,* 1867, Metropolitan Museum of Art, New York

Manet, *The Battle of the Kearsarge and the Alabama,* 1864, Johnson Collection, Philadelphia Museum of Art, Philadelphia

Like Géricault with his *Raft of the Medusa*, nineteenth-century artists often filled the role of picture journalists, recording the dramatic events of the day, sometimes showing the large works in exhibitions for a ticket-buying public. In 1864 Manet was stirred by a foreign war that came close to home. The Confederate raider *Alabama*, which had been successful in disrupting Union trade with Europe, was finally trapped off Cherbourg by the frigate *Kearsarge* and sunk. Advance publicity of the impending battle was such that hotels with a water view were in demand. Manet's version of the battle added a French boat in the foreground, heading out to rescue survivors.

With a little juggling of history and geography, one could imagine the encounter taking place near Le Havre, where Monet painted his parents on the *Terrace at Sainte-Adresse*. Civilization had not yet advanced to the point where the Monets could watch a war on TV while enjoying the sea breeze, so I decided to provide them with one.

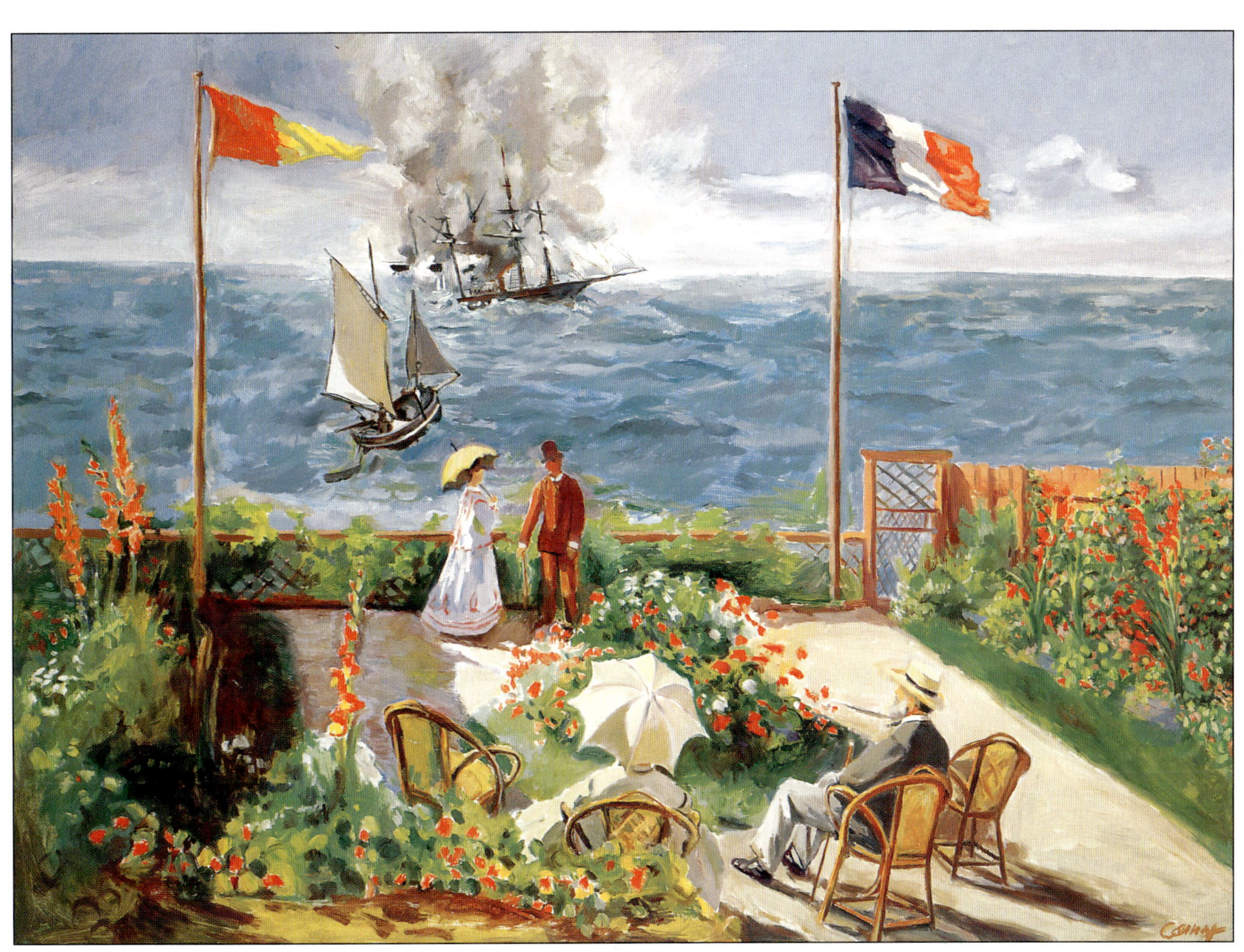

Duet for Charlotte Moorman

1989, 30 x 40 inches

Sources

Degas, *Woman Combing her Hair,* 1887–90, Musée d'Orsay, Paris

Degas, *The Dance Lesson* (detail), 1877–78, Havemeyer Collection, New York

I began this while Charlotte Moorman, the courageous, sometimes topless, cellist, tireless champion of the avant-garde, sidekick of Nam June Paik, and sometime collaborator of mine, was still among us. Now it is my tribute to her inspiring memory.

I first met Charlotte in 1970 when, as Assistant Director of the Rose Art Museum at Brandeis University, I organized the world's first museum exhibition of video art, called "Vision and Television." The impact of video art on these paintings cannot be exaggerated. Moving to New York, I worked as co-writer/narrator with Nam June and Charlotte on some video works for PBS, produced at WNET's experimental TV Lab. I went back on camera for a couple of years, hosting a series on video art called *VTR: Video and Television Review.* One day at the lab in 1975, working with the engineer John Godfrey, I improvised a video called *Be My Host.* As we played a videotape of one of my old Boston Museum programs, I electronically joined my earnest, younger self, wryly commenting on those years and walking in and out of the paintings "he" was discussing. At the time, it seemed a self-indulgent, Norma Desmond–like ego trip, but it cleared a path that would eventually lead me back to my own studio, ready to try similar, hallucinatory image play in oil paint, so that characters from famous paintings could interact with one another just as freely.

The action of the woman combing her hair reminded me of a cellist in performance, so I borrowed a violinist from another Degas pastel to accompany her, appearing, of course, as if by chroma key.

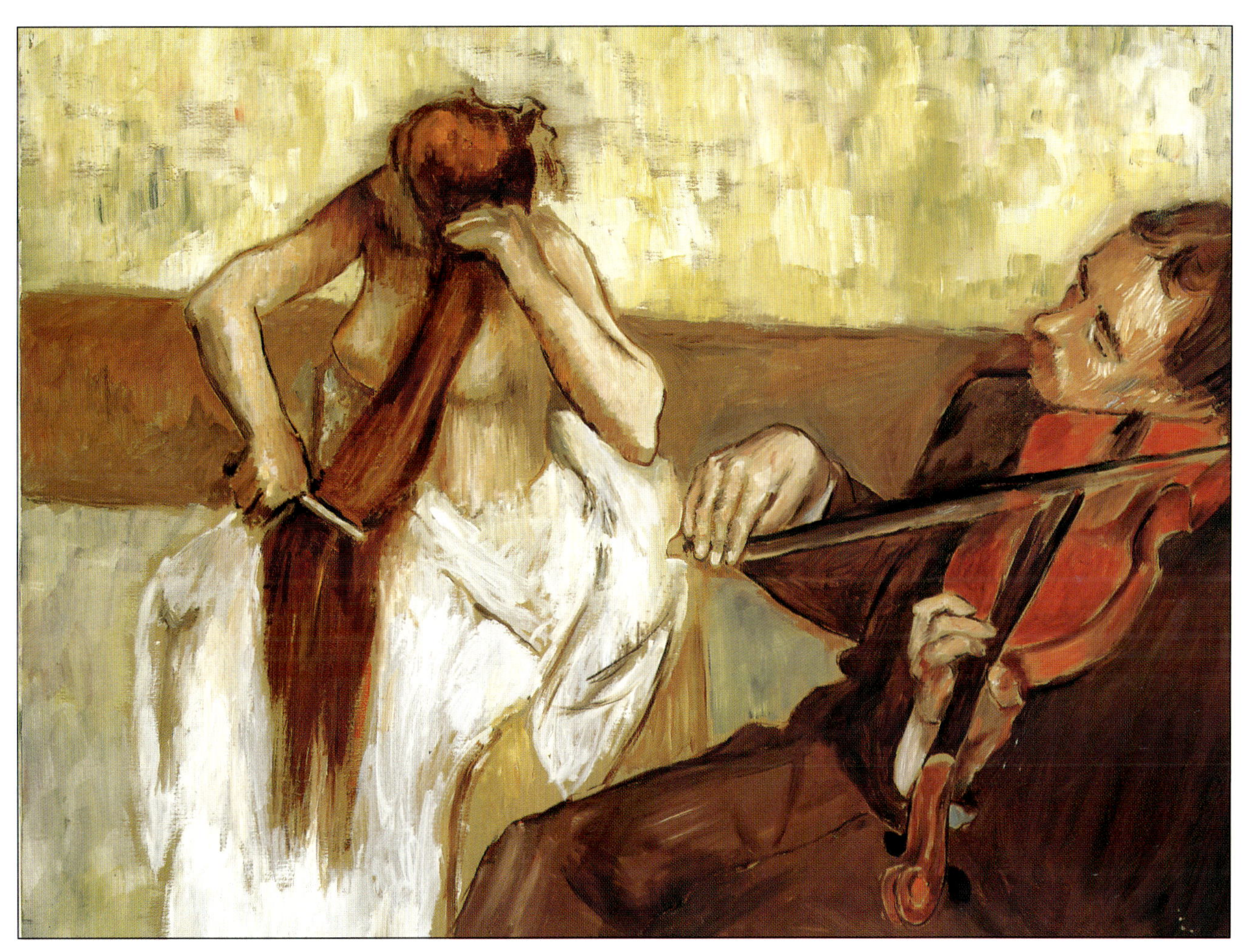

Ballad of the Working Girl

1989, 30 x 40 inches

Sources

Degas, *Two Laundresses,* 1884, Musée d'Orsay, Paris

Degas, *Café Singer,* 1878, Fogg Art Museum, Cambridge

For all of Degas's well-known flaws as a human being, he was often capable of works that move us with their unsentimental but sharp human empathy as well as their masterful observation. The laundress almost seems to sing out her weariness and her boredom, and here, another Degas working girl, from the popular café-concerts, picks up the tune.

I learned about empathy from Degas. At art school in Boston, the art history professor assigned first-year students to copy from a reproduction any master drawing we admired. I found a delicate Degas pencil drawing of a dancer standing on one foot, adjusting a slipper. When the professor came to my drawing, she held it up to the class and intoned, with all the considerable drama that she could summon, "This . . . is . . . Empathy." I gathered that this was somehow related to sympathy and, from her expression, probably not a bad thing to have. It wasn't until much later that I realized it can get you in a lot of trouble at parties, and on moonlit walks, and should probably be left at home when taking the New York subway.

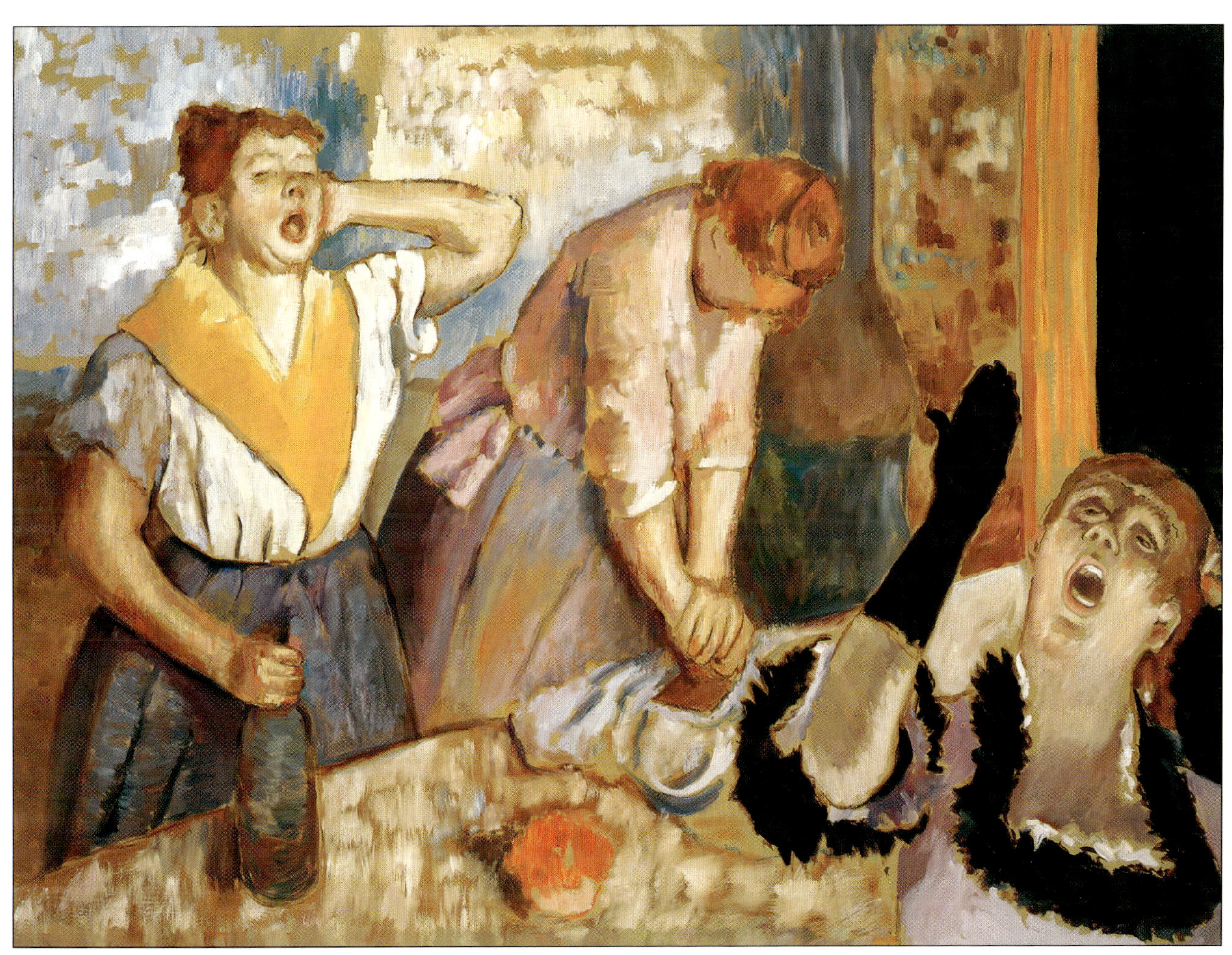

Dada Vinci

1990, 48 x 70 inches

Sources

Leonardo da Vinci, selected works

Duchamp, selected works

It's a rare occasion for me to accept a commission to paint a subject not of my choice, but the chance to introduce Leonardo da Vinci to Marcel Duchamp was irresistible. Amid sketches adapted from Leonardo's notebooks, I turned Duchamp's notorious urinal/sculpture into a planter, transformed his "ready-made" bottle-dryer into gold, as if by the artist's touch, and posed his drag alter ego, Rose Selavy, as the Mona Lisa. The arduous physical conditions imposed by the collector during the creation of this piece were of the kind that would have daunted many artists. I had to paint the work in the guest quarters adjoining her family's villa (they were away) near Cannes, in Mougins, where Picasso had his last studio. In between painting and dips in the shimmering, electronically cleaned, flower-encircled pool, I was forced to eat three exquisite gourmet meals a day on the terrace overlooking the bay, prepared by a cook trained in the finest cuisines of Provence and northern Italy. Would Van Gogh have stood for such treatment?

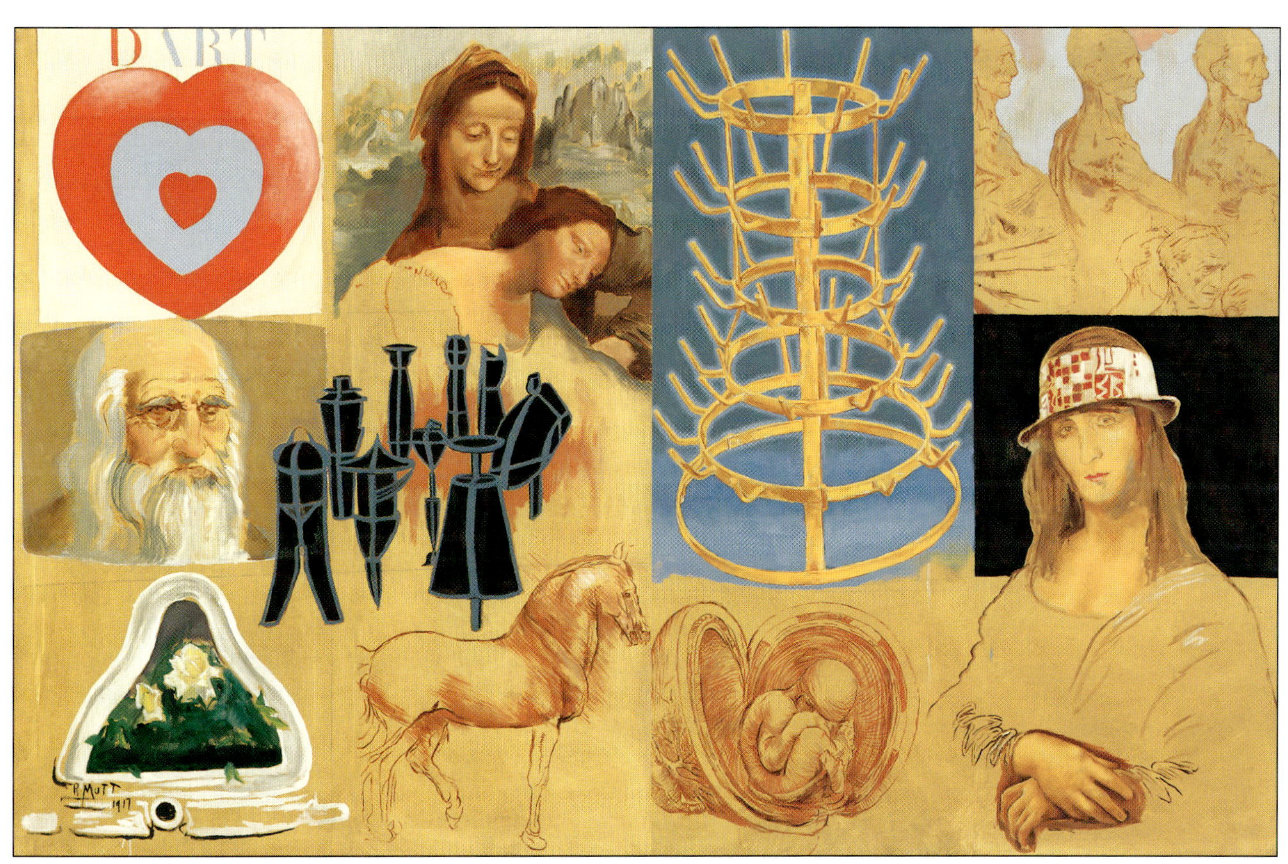
R.MUTT
1917

Hands Off the Polish Rider

1990–93, 68 x 64 inches

Sources

Rembrandt, *The Polish Rider,* 1655, Frick Collection, New York

Rembrandt, *Self-Portrait,* 1655, Kunsthistoriches Museum, Vienna

I was largely indifferent to the work of the Amsterdam-based Rembrandt Research Committee, who have been storming around the museums of the world for the past twenty years, driving museum directors up the wall as, one after another, they questioned the authenticity of each museum's "Rembrandt" treasures. According to the committee, the number of oil paintings actually by the master's hand, reputed by one expert to be in the seven hundreds early in the century, was closer to two hundred and fifty, and falling. When they cast doubt on the genuineness of *The Polish Rider* in New York's Frick Collection, they finally got me angry. It's far from the best Rembrandt, and the horse is pathetically thin; but it's a fine romantic image, and many of us have been fond of it since our student days. I decided to prove that it was authentic by creating a painting showing the master in the process of painting it. After all he'd done for me, I owed him that much.

Thinking *The New Yorker* might be amused, I submitted a photo of it with a deadpan story that *this* painting had recently been discovered in a basement in Pinsk. Art experts, I wrote, have concluded that it is an eyewitness portrait by Rembrandt's greatest student, Carel Fabritius, showing his teacher, palette in hand, pausing in his work on *The Polish Rider.* After turning the story into *New Yorker*ese, they printed it along with the painting in their anniversary issue of 1993 under the title *Back in the Saddle*. A descendant of Mr. Frick was absolutely delighted when she saw the news and called the director to inform him that the *Rider* had at last been proven beyond a doubt to be a genuine Rembrandt. This gentleman had the unhappy duty of informing her that it was a hoax perpetrated by an artist named Connor. Curators at the Frick enjoyed it and came to see it in my studio.

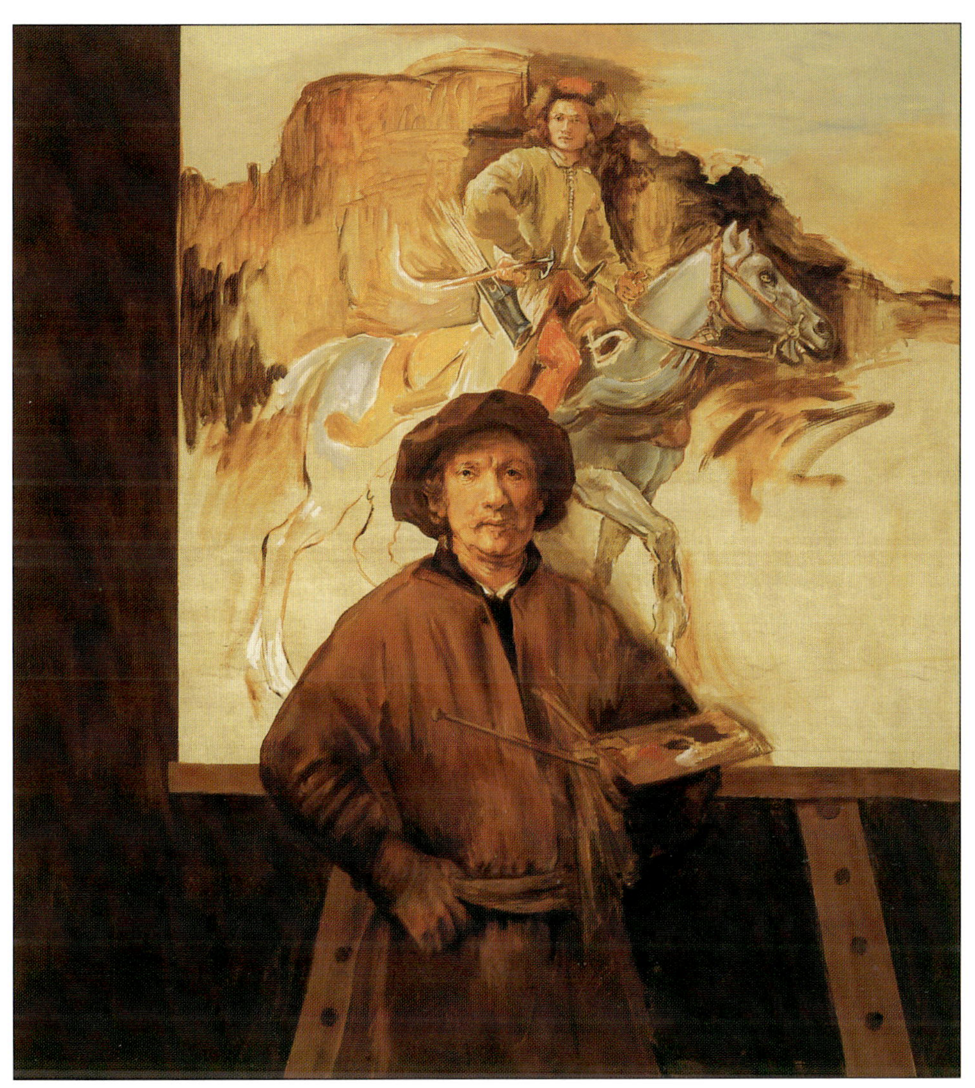

The New Art History

1990–93, 64 x 68 inches

Sources

Velasquez, *The Maids of Honor* (detail), 1656, Prado, Madrid

Velasquez, *Juan de Pareja,* 1650, Metropolitan Museum of Art, New York

Spurred, so to speak, by *The Polish Rider* into exploring further the problem of authenticity, I turned to a painting cloaked in mystery but whose authorship has never been in question. *The Maids of Honor,* by the seventeenth-century Spanish painter Velasquez, is widely regarded as one of the peaks of European art. My modest version simply points out that the artist's studio assistant, Juan de Pareja, immortalized by Velasquez in the great portrait in the Metropolitan, was himself a painter and was seen wielding brushes in the vicinity of the *Maids* while it was in progress. Most likely, he was just working nearby on his own painting and accidentally found himself in a position to add to the famous spatial and psychological ambiguity of Velasquez' masterpiece.

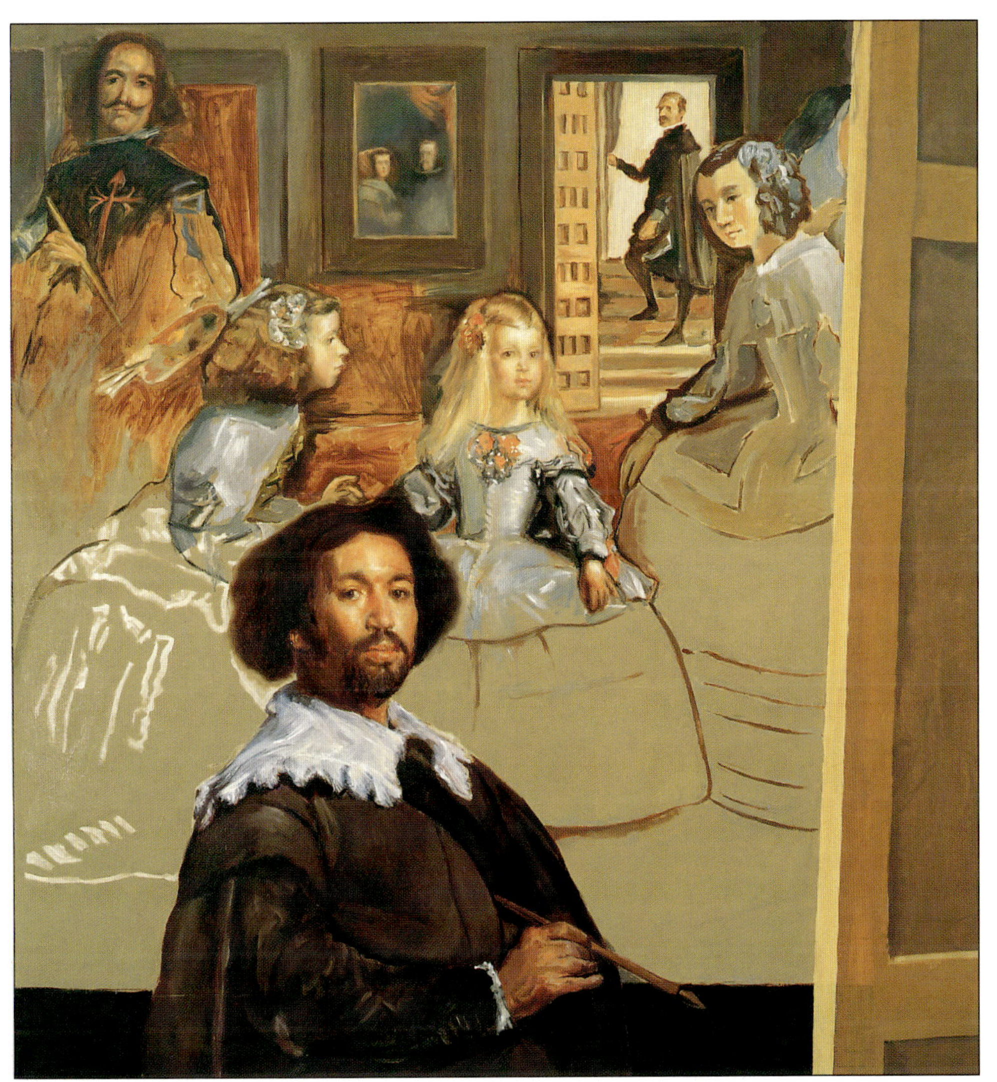

The Inquisitor and the Impostor (first stage)

1990, 64 x 68 inches

Sources

El Greco, *The Grand Inquisitor,* Cardinal Niño de Guevara (?), 1596–1600

El Greco, *Portrait of an Elderly Gentleman,* 1590–1600, Metropolitan Museum of Art, New York

They hung together in the Metropolitan for decades, the intimidating *Grand Inquisitor,* Cardinal Niño de Guevara, by El Greco, next to a small self-portrait of the artist himself. That's the image we, as students, had of the master of Toledo, the high-domed, mournful-eyed painter of dramatic, attenuated religious figures, gazing soulfully toward heaven. More recent scholarship concluded it's not the old Greek himself, but some stranger. The label now reads, "Portrait of an Elderly Gentleman" by El Greco. This identity mix-up inspired the following flight of fancy.

The cardinal decides he needs a portrait of himself to confirm his exalted position in the eyes of the people. "Who's the best?" he asks. "El Greco," say his bishops. "Tell the captain of the guard to bring him at once, with his brushes and paints." So the guards mistakenly roust out of bed this old guy who *looks* like the artist and drag him down to the castle. He's a tailor who paints on the side, but he's too frightened to confess that he's not El Greco. I sympathized with his plight, not being El Greco either.

This is the first stage of the painting, or what I think of as the Saint Agnes version, after the parish in Arlington, Massachusetts, where my family's house was spiritually annexed by the surrounding church, convent, and parochial school. The "impostor's" situation reminded me of facing the priest after absentmindedly ringing so many bells at Mass that the congregation seemed to be playing musical chairs. I had never heard of an altar boy being burned at the stake, and I didn't *want* to hear of one, so I turned in my cassock and surplice and rejoined the secular community.

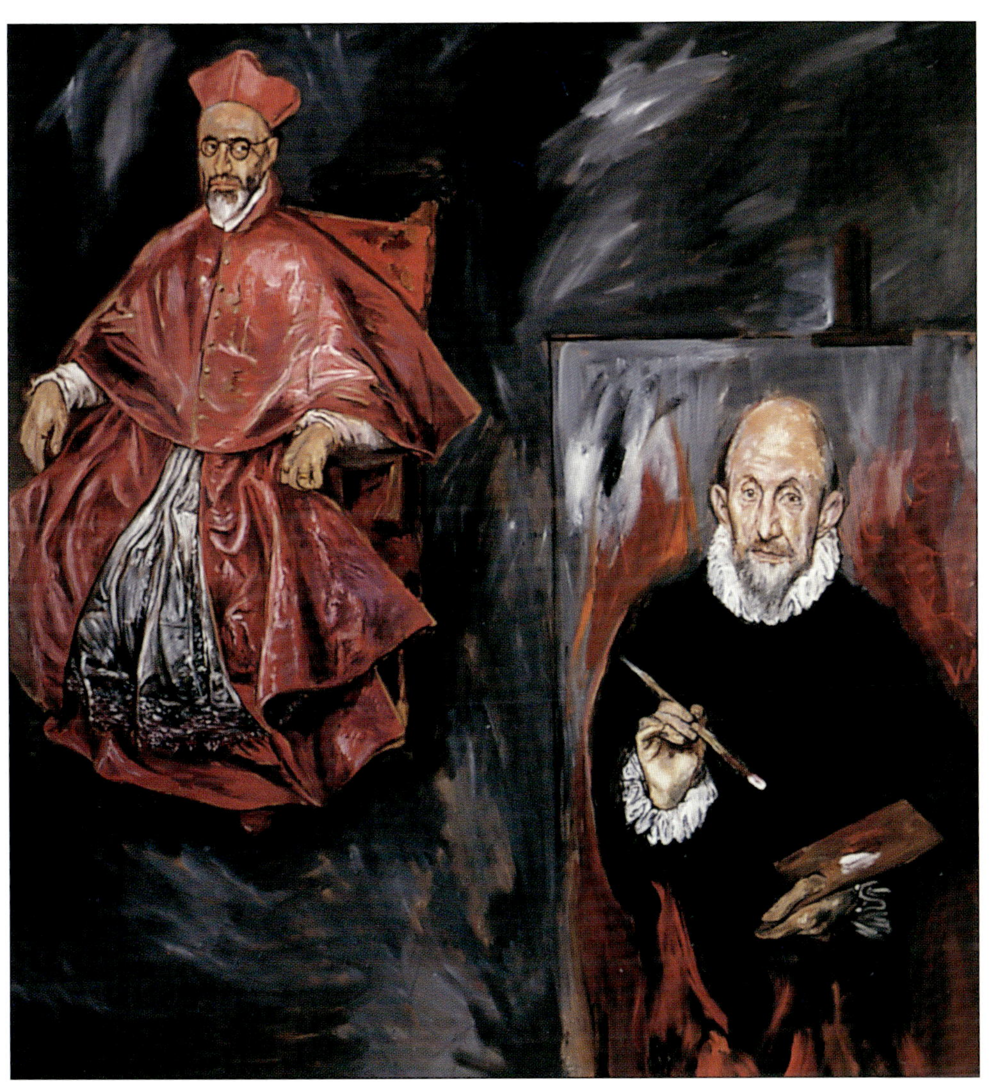

The Inquisitor and the Impostor

1990, 64 x 68 inches

Sources

El Greco, *The Grand Inquisitor,* Cardinal Niño de Guevara (?), 1596–1600

El Greco, *Portrait of an Elderly Gentleman,* 1590–1600, Metropolitan Museum of Art, New York

Perhaps I had been too hasty in prejudging what the unwilling impostor's fate would be. I decided to let him show what he could do, before he got sent to the dungeon. Like El Greco himself, he turns out to have a surprisingly modern style, although probably not what the cardinal had in mind to inspire the populace. Art historians, who got him into this muddle in the first place by their incorrect identification, may yet save him from the wrath of the inquisitor. The latest scholarship suggests there may be *two* impostors in this painting. Research now reveals that the severe-looking cardinal may not be the inquisitor at all, but another prince of the church, who had a great reputation as an enlightened patron of the arts. He might even like modern art.

The hands, brushes, and palette were borrowed from an El Greco painting of his artist son.

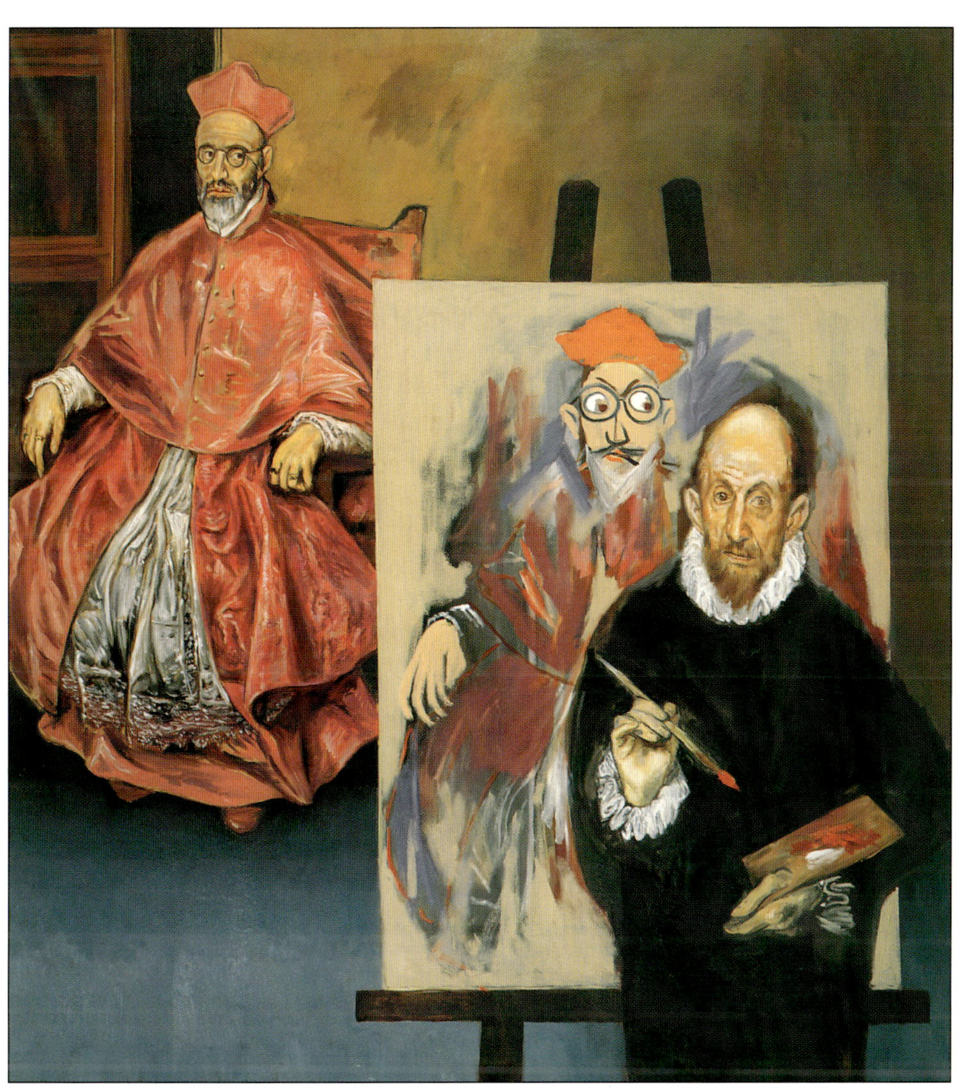

Paco Si, Goya No

1990, 64 x 68 inches

Source

Goya's Workshop, *Majas on a Balcony*, c.1811, Metropolitan Museum of Art, New York

When the Metropolitan Museum announced that its beloved *Majas on a Balcony* by Goya was *not* by Goya but was only a workshop version (the original is in a private Swiss collection), feelings of chagrin were noted even as far as my house. After all, believing it was by Goya, I had copied part of it in *The Spanish Visitors* (page 55). What has the world come to when you can't even be sure you're stealing from an original? I decided to take a positive approach and say, if not Goya, who?

It occurred to me that those mysterious fellows lurking in the background must have been posed for by assistants in the workshop, and one of them, let's say it was Paco, the shy one on the right hiding his face, may have made this version.

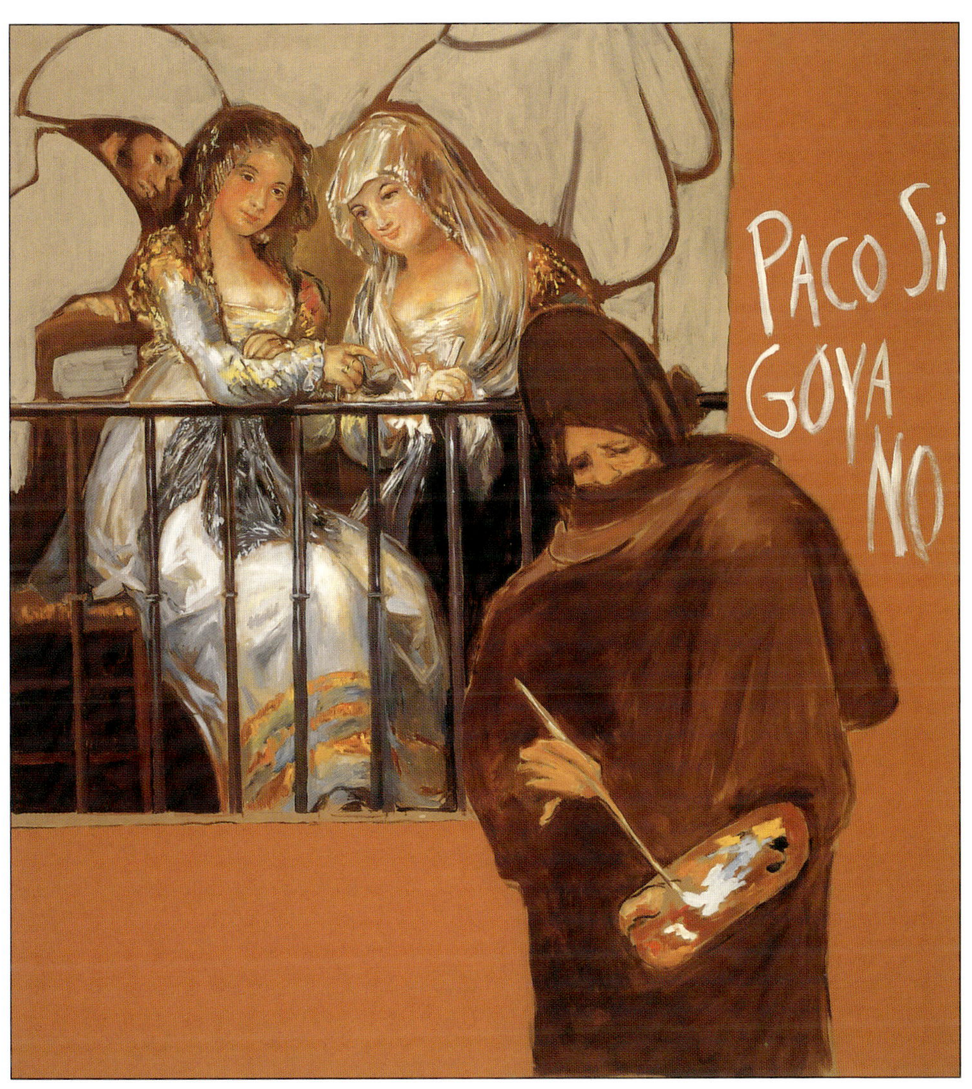
PACO SI
GOYA
NO

Art Is Not Funny

1990, 64 x 68 inches

Sources

Leonardo da Vinci, *Self-Portrait,* 1514–19, Royal Library, Turin

Duchamp, *L.H.O.O.Q.,* 1919, private collection, Paris

This reunion of the dynamite da Vinci/Duchamp duo was inspired by study of the wonderful self-portrait drawing that Leonardo made as an old man. Why, I wondered, does he look so *angry?* Fate, of course, had provided him with a few reasons, including the physical destruction or disintegration of some of his most important works during his lifetime. Perhaps his spirit has somehow become aware of what has happened to art *since* his time, especially in the twentieth century, when a nihilistic irony and disrespect for the achievements of the past have been rampant. Who would be the most likely target of his fury if not the Dadaist Duchamp, who had the boldness to draw a moustache on a poster of the *Mona Lisa* and to write an indecent French pun beneath it? Any museum in town would find a spot in its lecture series for *The Return of Leonardo,* ready to show slides of irreverent modern work, condemn its frivolity, and argue for a return to sanity.

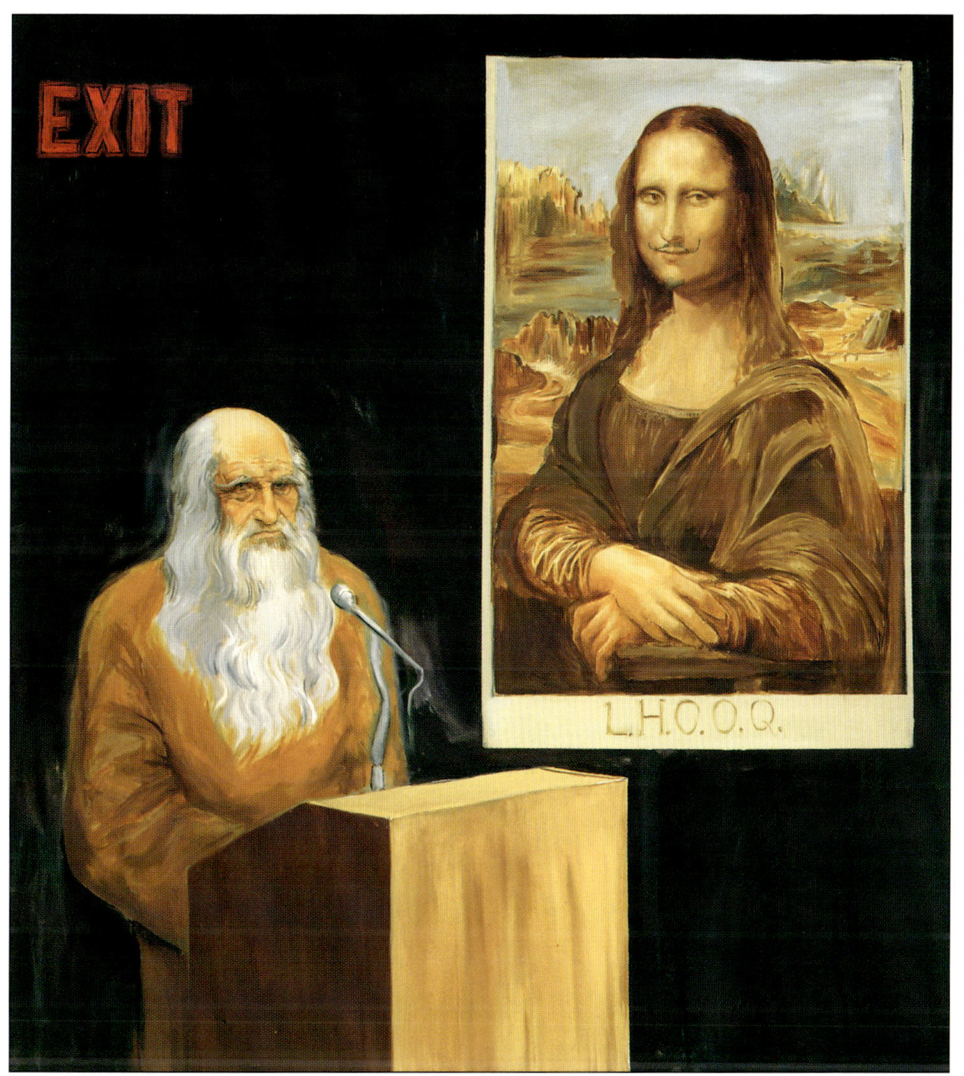
EXIT
L.H.O.O.Q.

Goya's Dream

1990, 48 x 60 inches

Sources

Goya, *Self-Portrait,* 1815,
Academy of Fine Arts, Madrid

Goya, details from selected works

Fantastic visions and nightmares came readily to Goya's mind after he witnessed the horrors of the war between France and Spain. My fantastic vision saw Goya presenting slides of his work to the Madrid Art Association. The nightmare, familiar to artists who have shown slides of their precious creations in similar circumstances, is that the slides are disorganized, out of order, upside down, or, in this extreme case, bunched up in the same slot in the projector. The result is like a collage, featuring most prominently a combination of his two notorious paintings of the Duchess of Alba, one nude and the other clothed.

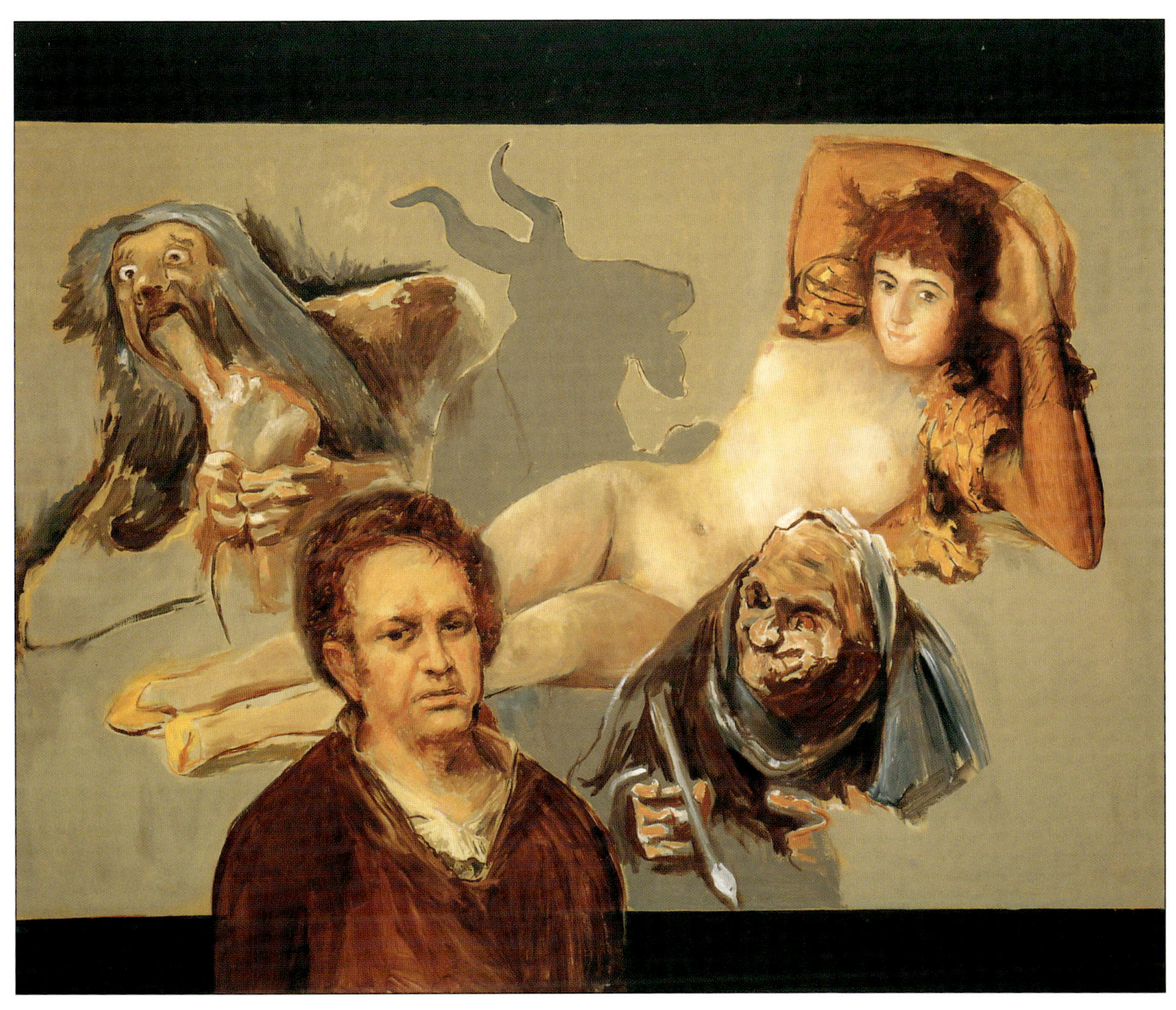

The Cooking of French Art

1991, 32 x 30 inches

Sources

Watteau, *Gilles* (detail), 1718, Louvre, Paris

Manet, *A Bar at the Folies-Bergère*, 1882, Courtauld Institute, London

Full frontal French. A little like Pinkie and Blue Boy of the *Royal Wedding* (page 57), Suzon and Gilles seemed to reach out to each other across time. Changing the chapeau of Gilles (the figure from Commedia dell'Arte in Watteau's famous painting) to a chef's hat, puts them both at work in a French restaurant or perhaps in a fancy catering service. The menu they are offering at the moment seems to be exclusively alcoholic, but I couldn't resist using the title of one of my old television programs from the Museum of Fine Arts in Boston.

Museum Open House was broadcast immediately following the hugely popular cooking show with Julia Child, co-author of *The Art of French Cooking*. Once, I thought we might gather in some unsuspecting members of her audience if we went directly, without opening titles, to a table full of the ingredients for making a painting: pigments, linseed oil, turpentine, and brushes. I stood behind in an apron, grinding pigments while cheerfully chatting about the recipe for an eighteenth-century French still life by Chardin, made, of course, with a simple brown sauce (the artist actually described the secret of his technique in those words). Then appeared the titles "*Museum Open House* with Russell Connor—*The Cooking of French Art*." It was hard to maintain the inspired level established by the title, but we made a few useful points along the way.

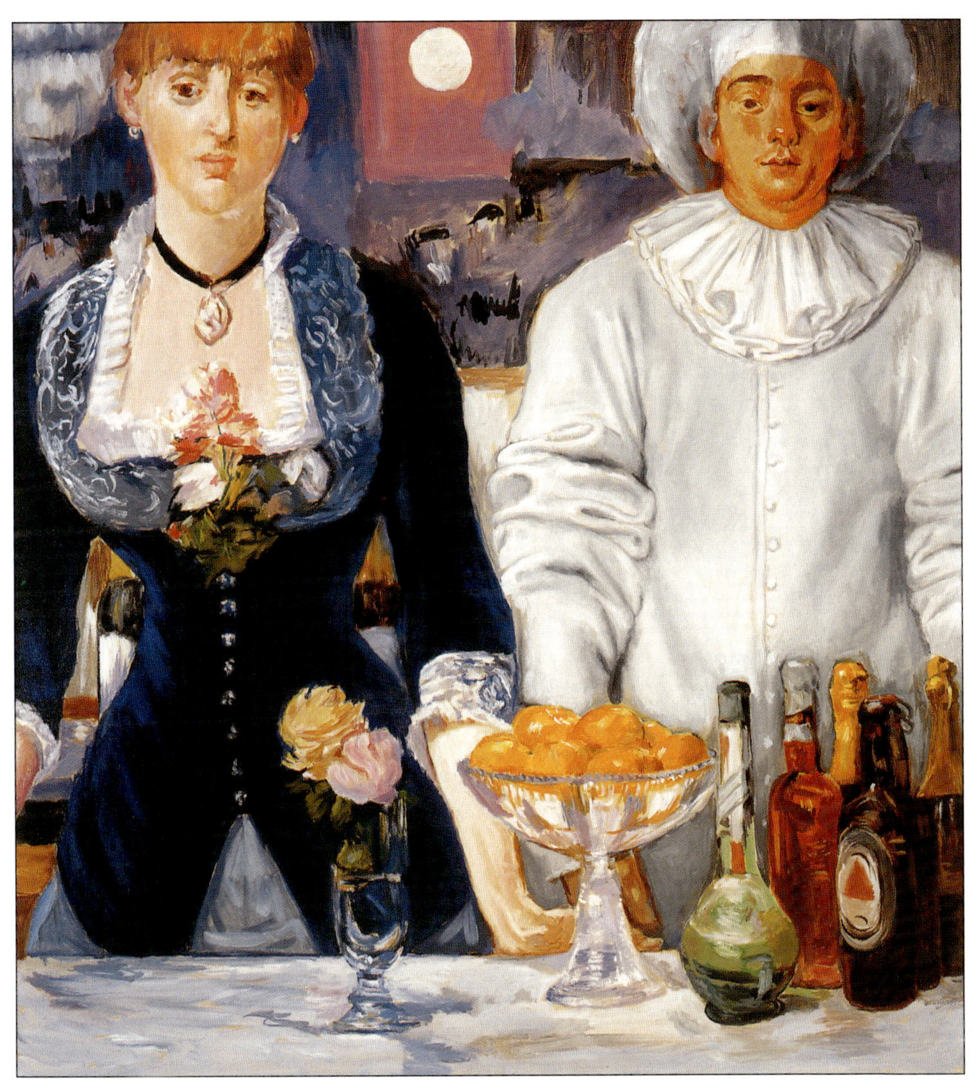

Planned Parenthood

1991, 48 x 48 inches

Source

Raphael, *Madonna del Granduca,* 1515, Pitti Palace, Florence

The T-shirt series grew from a desire to combine words and images. Like it or not, the T-shirt has become a universal mode of communication, and its simple form provided me with a chance to use broad, flat areas of color. They are oil or acrylic on canvas, and there's no plan to actually print them on T-shirts.

No offense is here intended, except perhaps to those who think they are acting in a religious spirit by harassing young women at clinics where they go to exercise their personal freedom. I thought it might be a useful reminder that Jesus Christ, whose cause they claim to champion, was known for his compassion above all else and would not likely be indifferent to the sight of more and more hungry, endangered, unwanted, and unloved children being brought into the world.

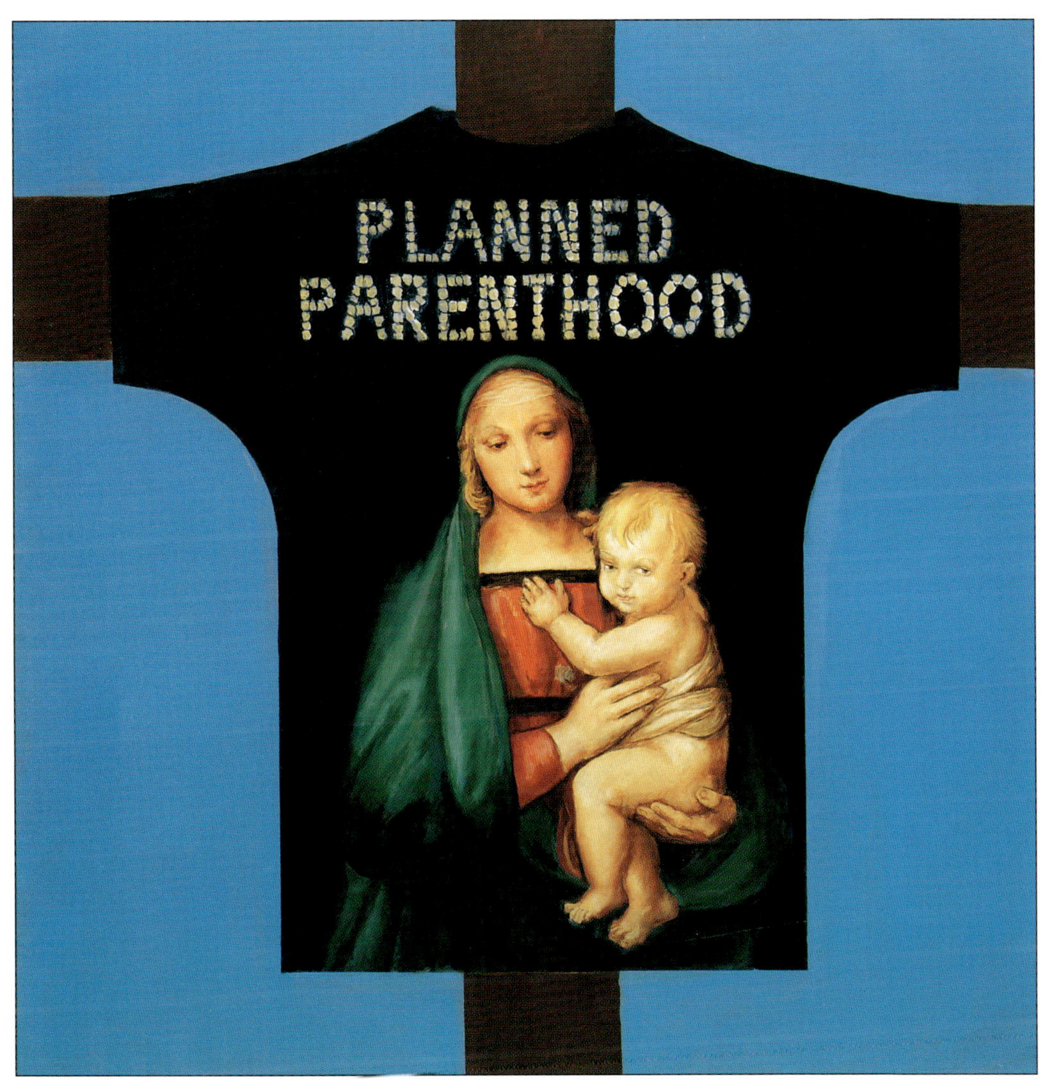
PLANNED
PARENTHOOD

Right to Life

1991, 48 x 48 inches

Source

Picasso, *Guernica* (detail), 1937, Prado, Madrid

An ironic companion to the previous work, with essentially the same message. Stories of children being killed by gangs in drive-by shootings were much in the news at the time.

I have great respect for artists with a passionate social conscience who feel compelled to express their anger on canvas, usually knowing that it will have little or no impact on the conditions they are protesting. Picasso's *Guernica*, for me the strongest painting of the twentieth century, stirred thousands of people but was no match for Franco and his Fascist allies.

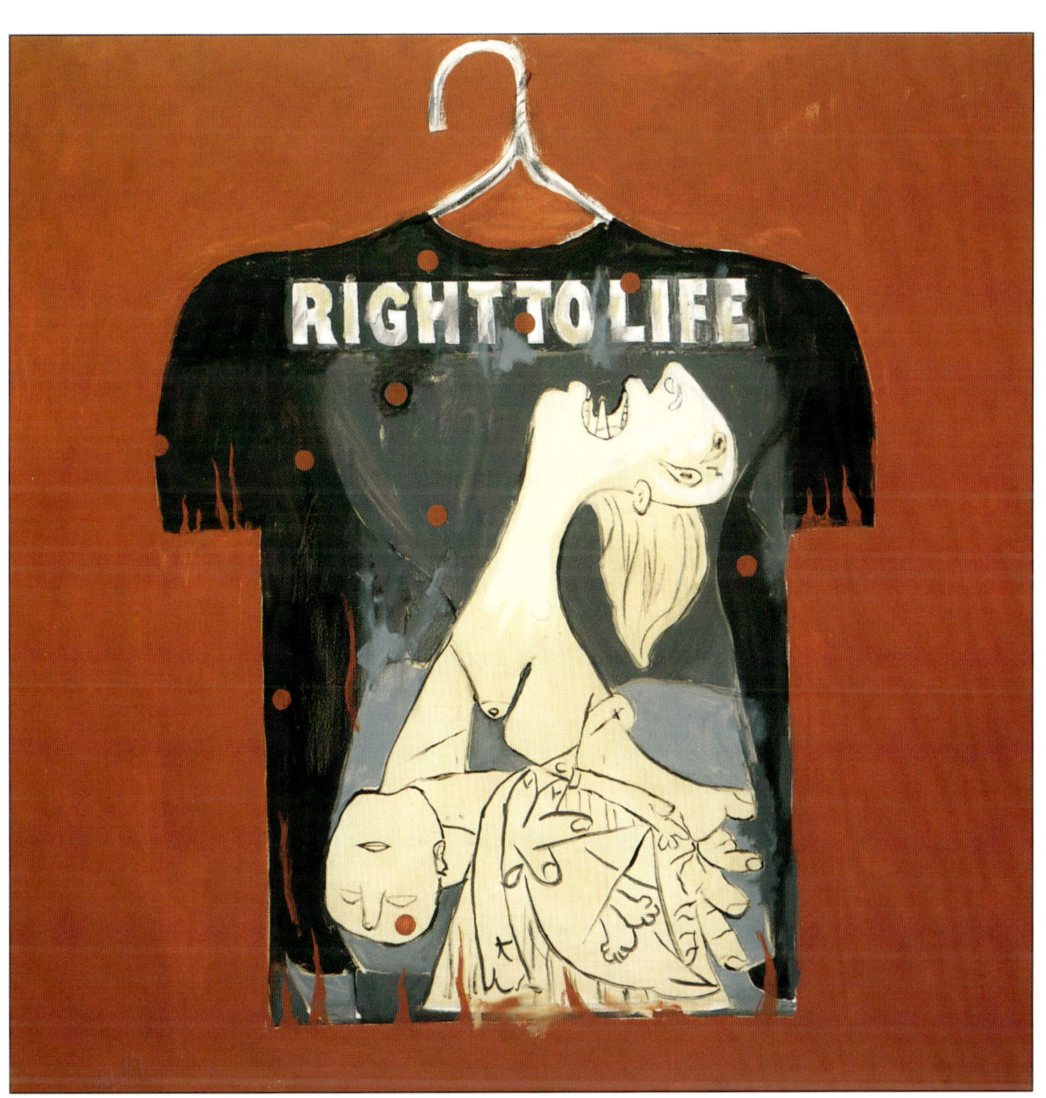
RIGHT TO LIFE

One Day at a Time

1992, 46 x 48 inches

Source

Caravaggio, *Bacchus,* 1593, Uffizi, Florence

Bacchus seemed to me the right poster boy to go with the slogan for Alcoholics Anonymous. Caravaggio, unlike members of AA, who are courageously combating the disease of alcoholism, was as self-destructive as he was creative. Rejecting both the handsome young Bacchus of antiquity and the grotesque Bacchus more familiar in his time, he selected a boy off the street, possibly a prostitute, and adorned him as the god of wine.

Caravaggio, who apparently never met a temptation he didn't like, nevertheless produced a series of masterpieces that directly or indirectly inspired Rubens, Velasquez, Rembrandt, and Vermeer, among countless others.

Just as the works of art I use are well known through wide reproduction, the words I add to them are familiar, popular, or banal. One hopes that the jolt of their juxtaposition will strike new sparks. This one (also the title of a 1970s TV series) is really about temptation of all kinds.

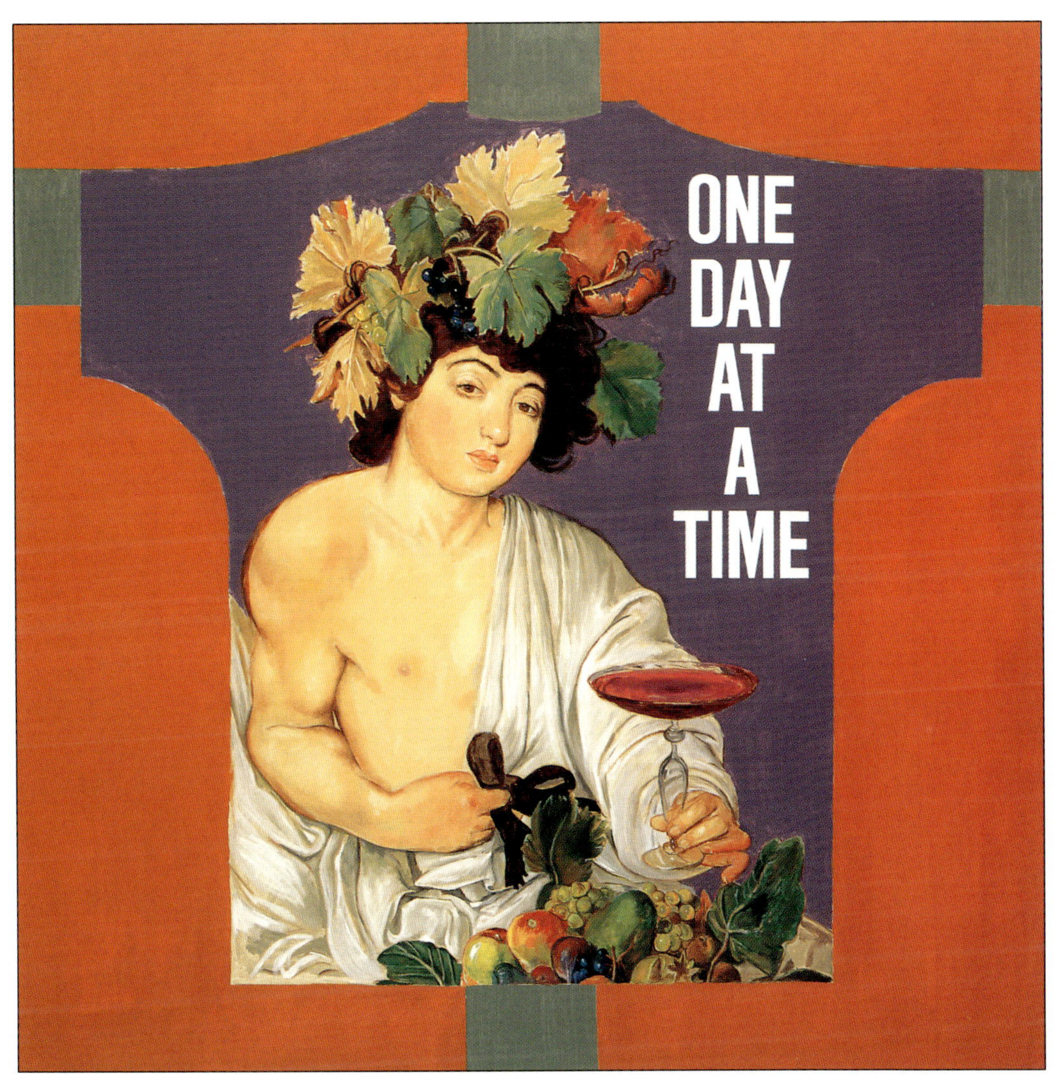
ONE
DAY
AT
A
TIME

Politically Correct

1992, 48 x 48 inches

Source

David, *Marat Assassinated,* 1793, Royal Museum of Fine Arts, Brussels

The now exhausted term "politically correct" has been for some time a club used by the Right to beat the Left, accusing it of sending out thought police to ensure righteous language and behavior in matters of race, gender, et cetera. I thought it would go nicely with Marat, who, when alive, exercised similar severity in judging who were true friends of the Revolution and who should visit Dr. Guillotine. The viewer may consider whether Marat was himself P.C., and if so, whether he attained that state before or after Charlotte Corday paid a fatal visit.

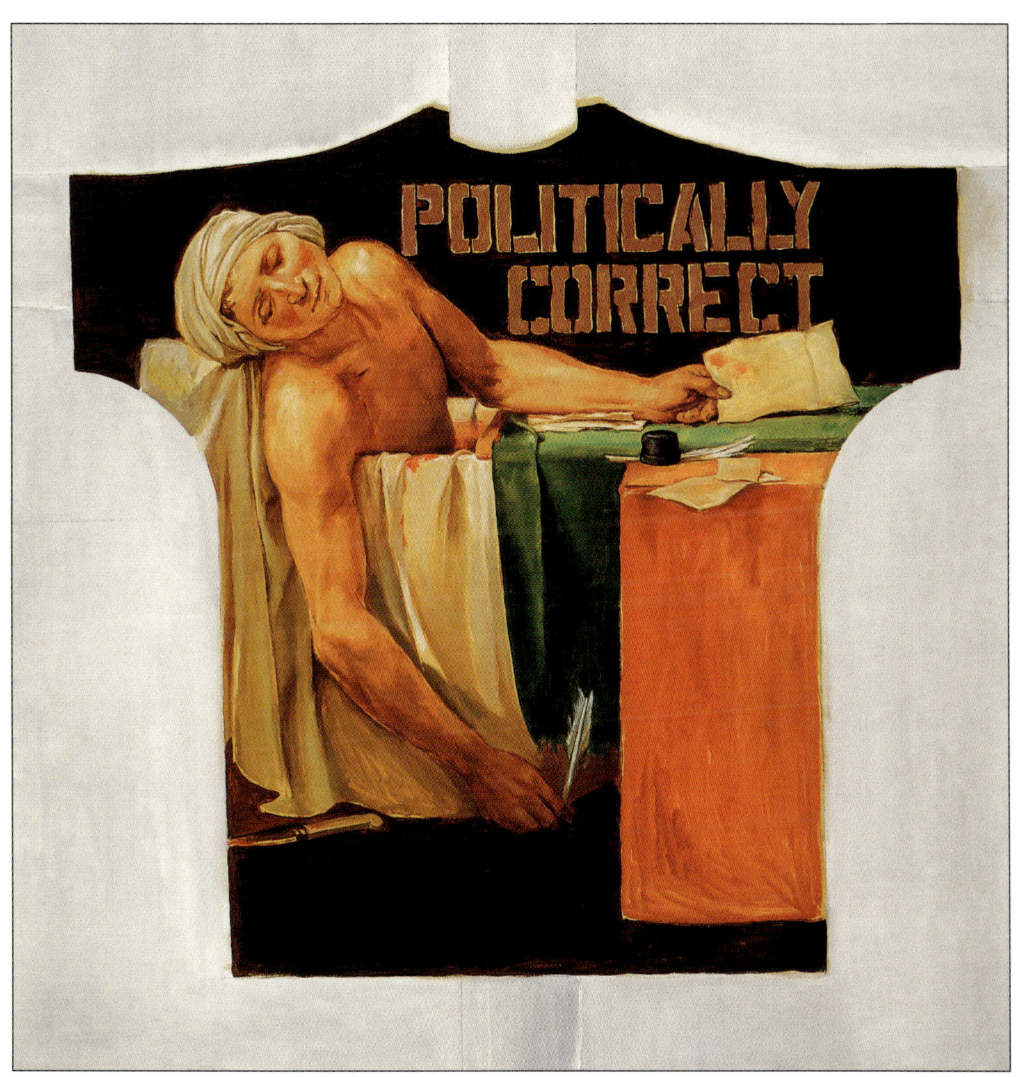
POLITICALLY
CORRECT

The New Yorker

1992, 48 x 48 inches

Source

Goya, *Beggar,* c.1824, Metropolitan Museum of Art, New York

Goya's tattered beggar might not conform to a New Yorker's sophisticated self-image, but he would not be out of place standing on my corner of Fifty-seventh Street, across the street from Carnegie Hall. He might do some good business with the out-of-town crowds that shuttle back and forth from the Hard Rock Cafe to Planet Hollywood to the Motown Cafe. The connections between the vaunted affluence of the high-rolling eighties, the downsizing of the nineties, and the massive increase of derelicts in New York City are complicated on paper but tragically clear on the sidewalks.

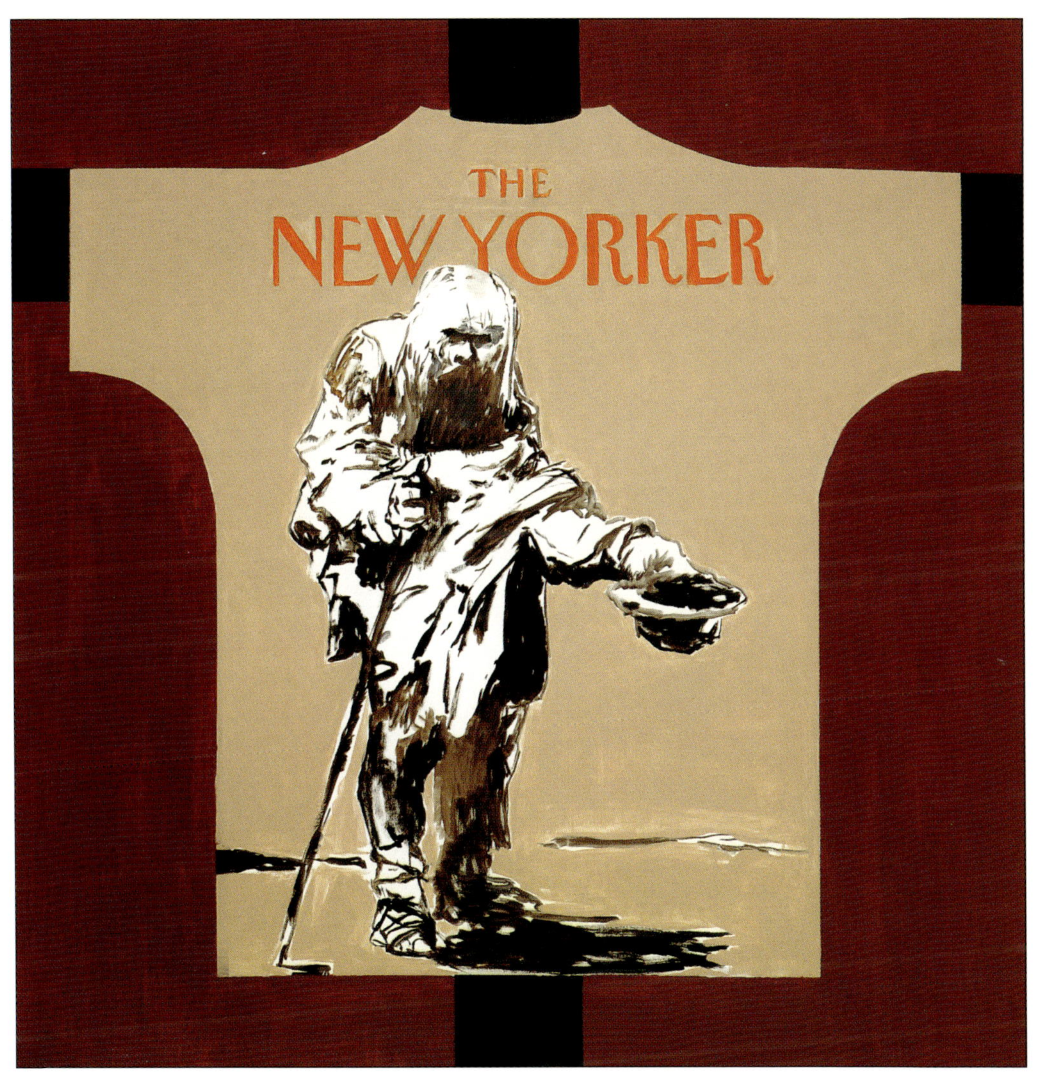
THE
NEW YORKER

When Art Was Art

1993, 72 x 68 inches

Source

Rembrandt, *Self-Portrait,* 1652, Kunsthistoriches Museum, Vienna

Obviously I never tire of this gentleman's face, and here, once again without permission, I use him in a message painting. The message is clearly reactionary, lamenting that some find it necessary to belittle the achievement of great artists of the past in order to point out the unjust neglect of others. It also (gently, to be sure) mocks my own work, and that of other "appropriation" artists, raising the question of whether any art so slavishly dependent on copying the past could be in any way original and creative.

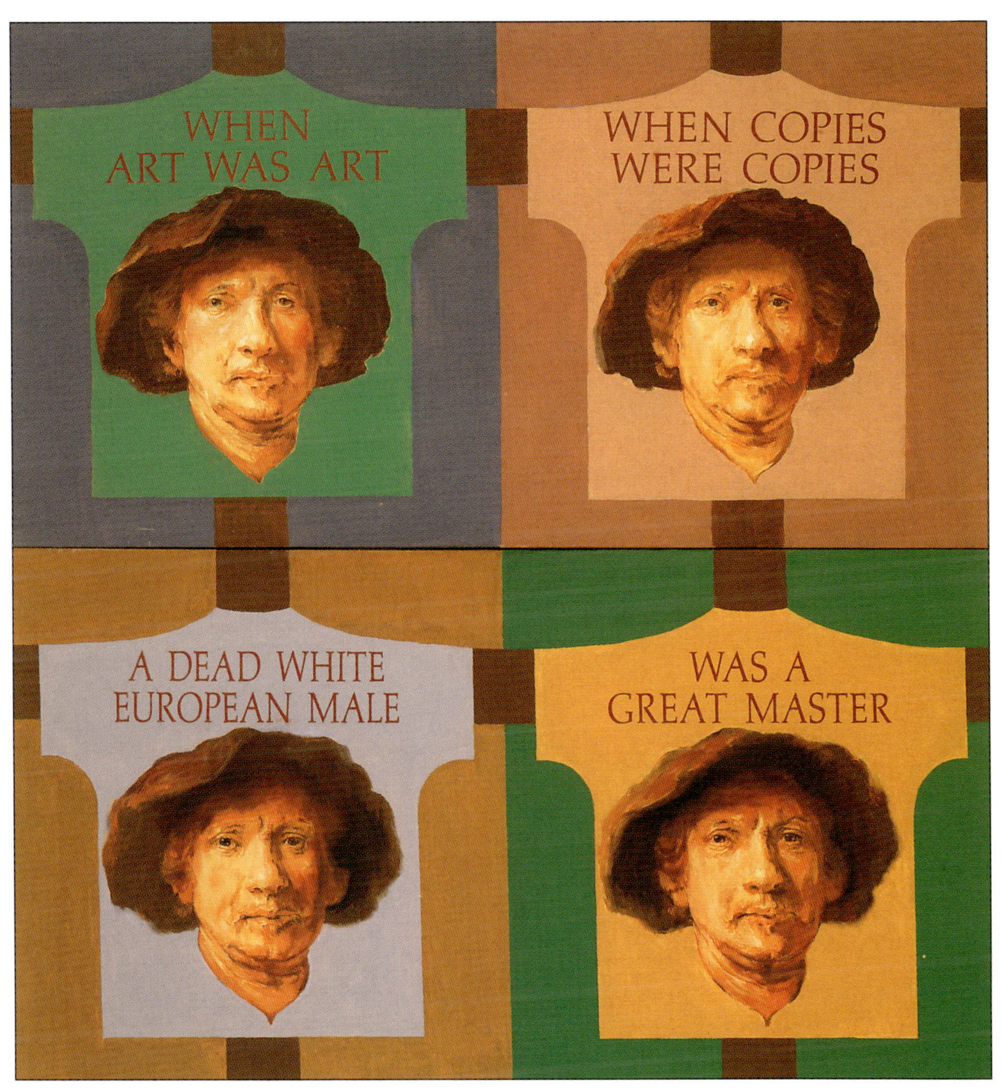
WHEN
ART WAS ART
WHEN COPIES
WERE COPIES
A DEAD WHITE
EUROPEAN MALE
WAS A
GREAT MASTER

Matisse, Not

1993, 48 x 48 inches

Source

Matisse, *Still Life with Oranges,* 1912, Musée Picasso, Paris

This painting was inspired by museum gift shops that, increasingly, feel free to put masterpieces on everything from scarves to place mats and T-shirts. It is a fact of our time that museums need these profitable outlets as other sources of support disappear. I consider my own aversion to this spectacle a blend of hypocrisy and elitism. It is certainly a phenomenon of our time that helps to make my work possible. Thinkers since Walter Benjamin have toiled with the question of what happens to art when the original "aura" is lost in the waves of mass reproduction. What appears to happen is that artists make a new subject of the aura itself.

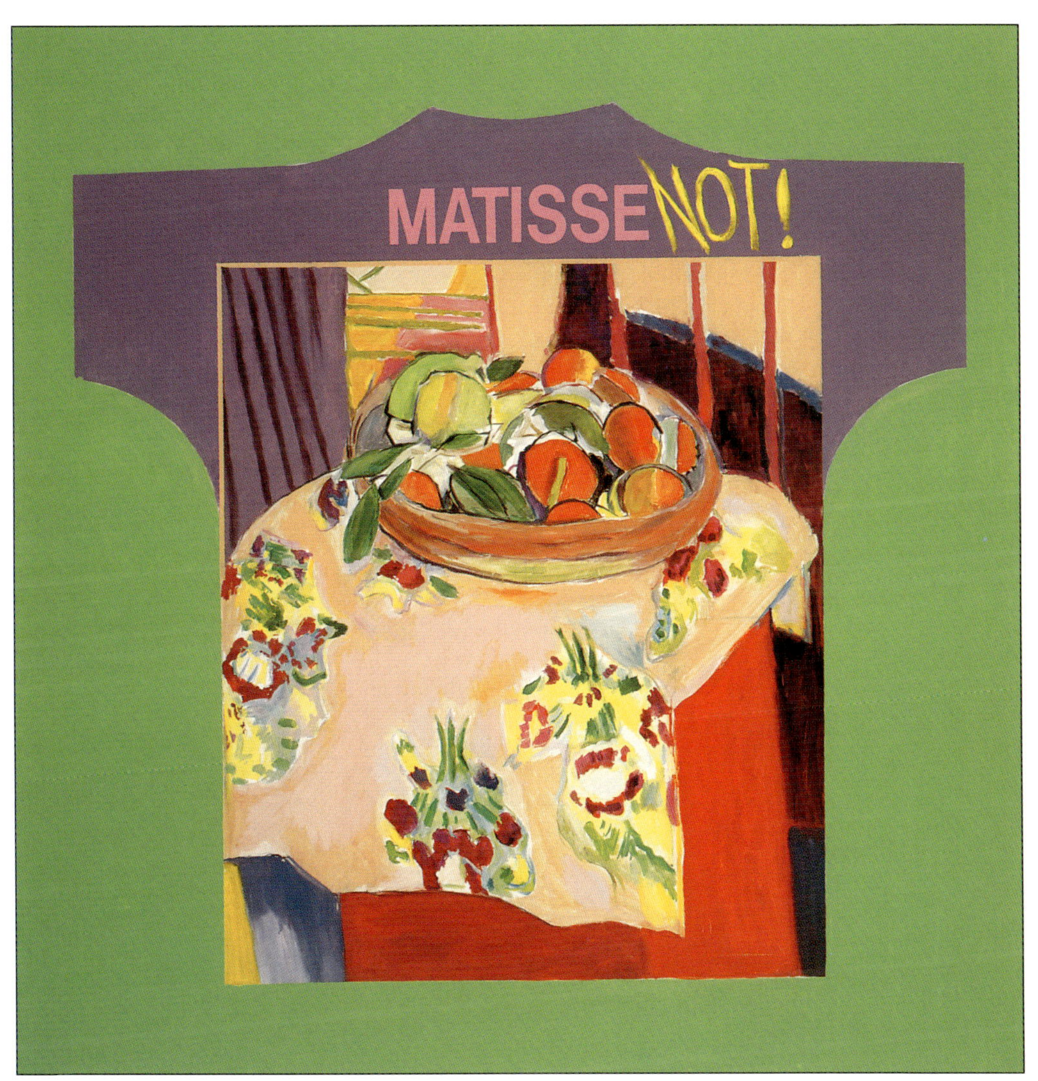
MATISSE NOT!

EuroDestiny

1992, 31 x 31 inches

Sources

Rembrandt, *Aristotle Contemplating the Bust of Homer,* 1653, Metropolitan Museum of Art, New York

Walt Disney, *Mickey Mouse,* 1928

When this was painted, I was in Paris and had worked up some indignation over the building of the EuroDisney wonderland southeast of the city. I wondered why France, the home of Mont Saint-Michel, the châteaus of the Loire Valley, and an abundantly rich history and culture, would need to import the prefabricated, special effects dreams of Disney. I was sure that its presence would be a deplorable influence on the rest of the old continent. Instead of Aristotle contemplating the bust of Homer, I pictured him pondering the bust of Mickey. So much for the artist as prophet. The European catastrophe turned out to be something much more serious called Bosnia, and EuroDisney had to be bailed out by a Saudi prince.

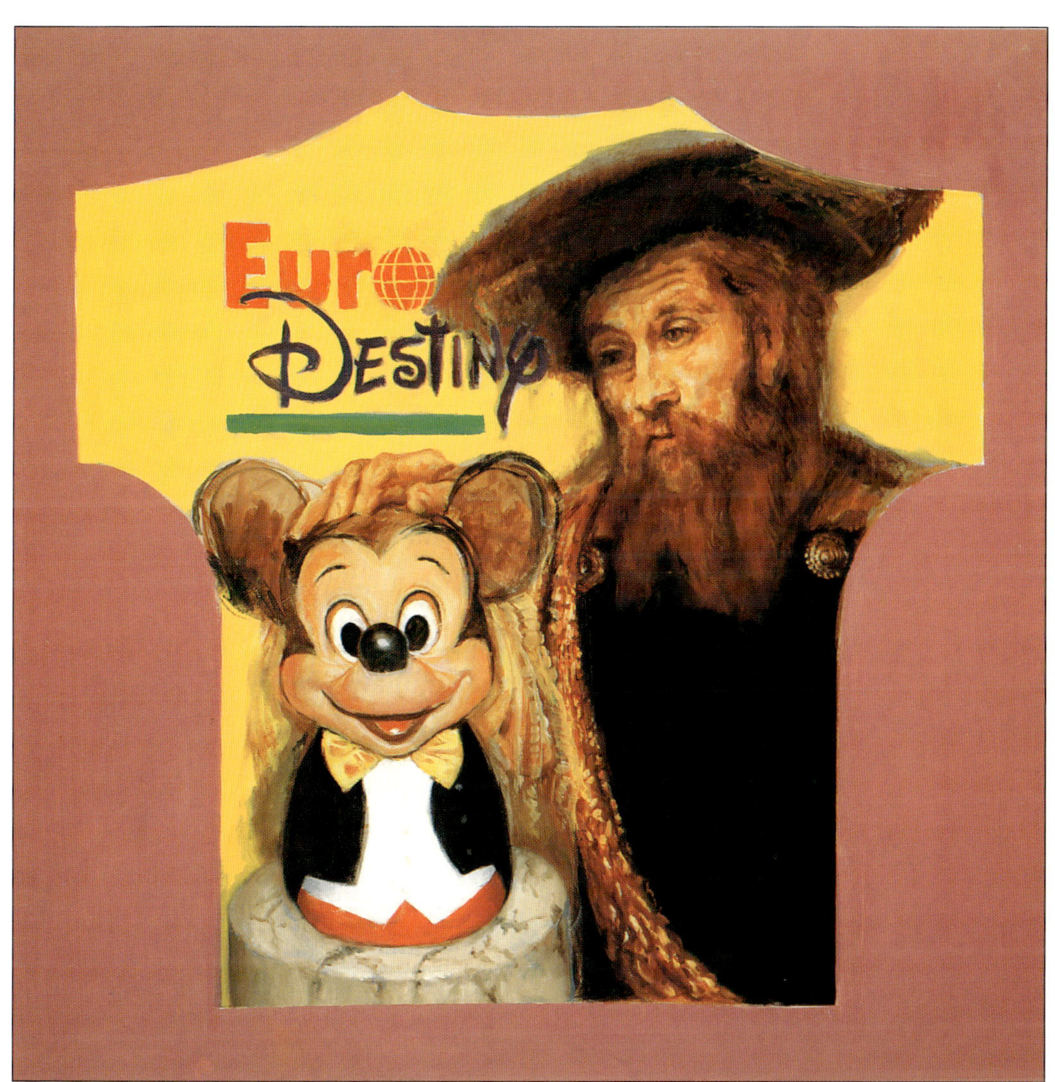
Euro
DESTINO

Dead White European Male

1993, 31 x 31 inches

Source

Van Gogh, *Self-Portrait,* 1889, private collection, Chicago

My first painting teacher, Patrick Gavin, said, "If you think that Van Gogh is the greatest artist who ever lived, you have a lot to learn about art. But if you are not deeply moved by his work, you probably don't know what art *is*." Genuine historical injustices and political agitation in academe have led students to protest the domination of our culture and our education by dead, white, European males. Curricula have been broadly revamped, and paranoid, die-hard Western culture supremacists have circled the wagons. No one, as far as I know, has asked that the beloved Van Gogh be removed from the museums, stricken from the history books, or deleted from the movies and CD-ROM, although the job of recalling the posters and postcards might reduce unemployment. I couldn't resist the irony of placing this tag on a man who was himself the quintessential outsider.

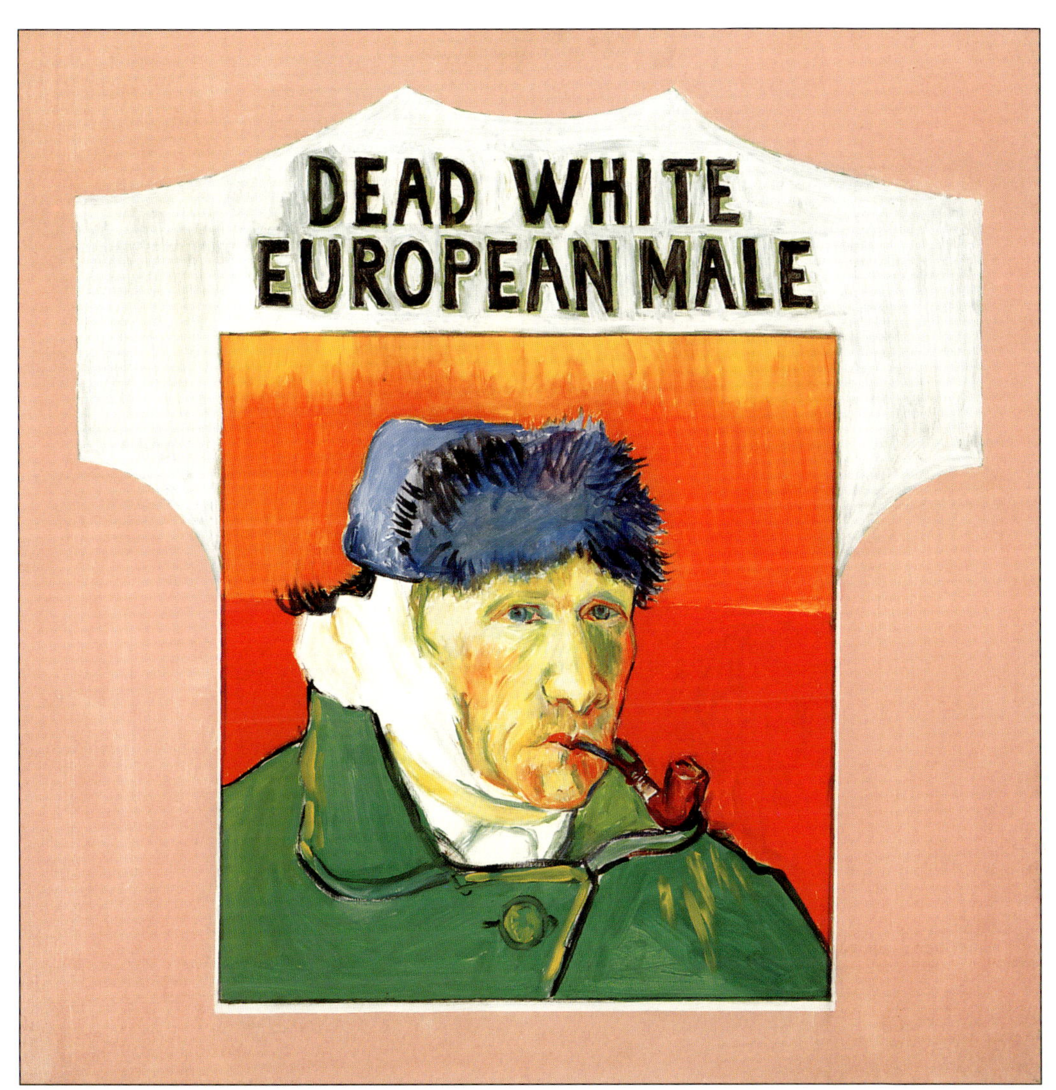
DEAD WHITE
EUROPEAN MALE

Combattez La Violence

1993, 31 x 31 inches

Source

Daumier, *The Robbery* (detail), 1858, Musée d'Orsay, Paris

The years I've spent in France may have earned me the right to unaffectedly title a work in French. The English version is a little tougher, *Kill Violence*. It's as exaggerated a statement as I can make about the murderous cycles of war, revenge, crime, and capital punishment. I learned about violence in the schoolyard, but my first introduction to poverty, to the tragedy, comedy, and sometime nobility of life among the downtrodden, came from art: from Daumier, Goya, Kollwitz, and those Americans who found their subjects in the Depression. Here, Daumier was depicting simple assault and robbery. It's been lamented that he would have been a greater artist if he drank less, but he's been great enough for me since I discovered him in high school and aspired to be the Daumier of the Boston subway.

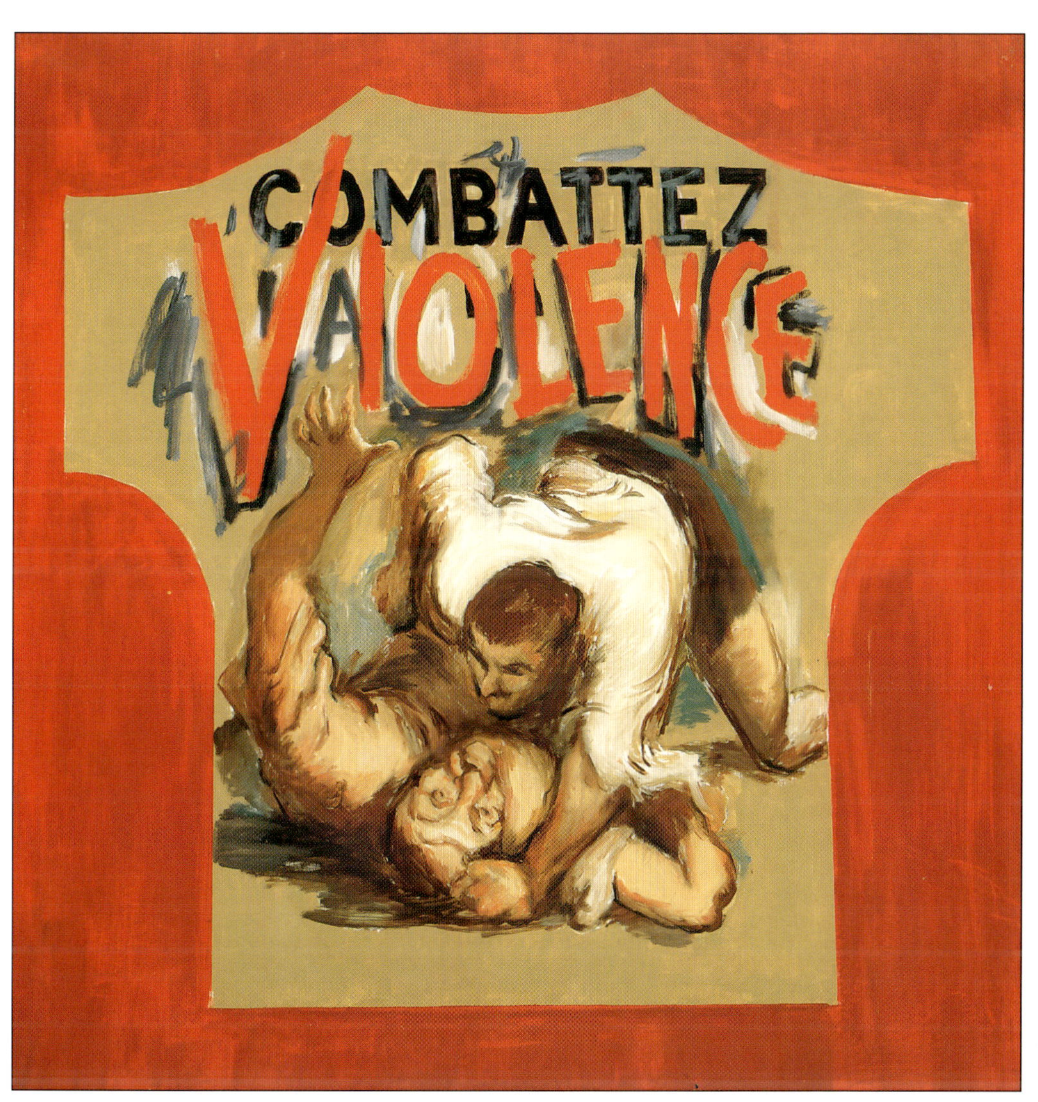
COMBATTEZ
VIOLENCE

Repent/Repaint

1994, 31 x 31 inches

Source

Michelangelo, *The Last Judgment* (detail), 1536–41, The Vatican, Rome

The recent high-risk cleaning and restoration of Michelangelo's frescos in the Sistine Chapel have given the restorers reason to deplore the repainting of their predecessors and have led others to doubt the wisdom of *their* touching the works. Any artist who has ever ruined a painting by working over it excessively understands "repent repaint." The approaching millennium, sure to bring out some who believe it means the end of the world ("Repent! The End is Near!"), gives this a nice topical touch.

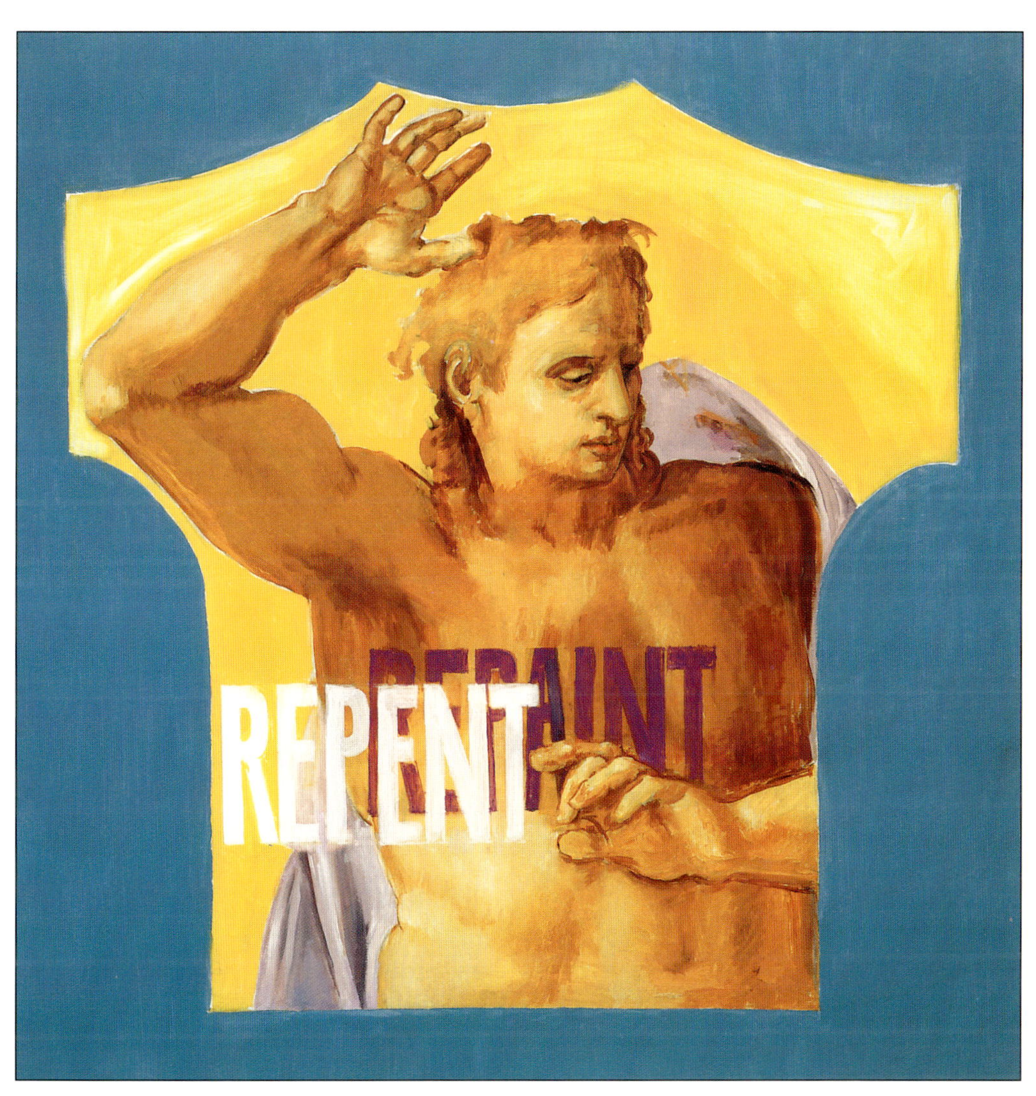
REPENT
REPAINT

I Don't Know, Vincent, What Do *You* Want to Do Tonight? (first stage)

1986, 40 x 30 inches

Sources

Gauguin, *Self-Portrait,* 1888, Vincent Van Gogh Museum, Amsterdam

Van Gogh, *The Café Terrace on the Place du Forum, Arles, at Night,* 1888, Kroller-Mueller Museum, Otterlo, The Netherlands

For all the drama of Paul Gauguin's two-month stay in Arles with Vincent Van Gogh, we know of no image of him there, neither painting nor fading photograph. To correct this historical oversight, I used a self-portrait that Gauguin had made as part of an exchange with Van Gogh (in which he had likened himself and fellow artists to "Les Miserables") and placed him in front of the terrace café that was the subject of a famous work by Vincent.

I thought of other old boys standing on street corners and used as the title a classic bit of dialogue from the 1955 Oscar-winning film *Marty,* written by Paddy Chayefsky and starring Ernest Borgnine. Gauguin addresses the question to us, or the "camera," as if we were Vincent. I felt something was still missing and put this unfinished painting aside.

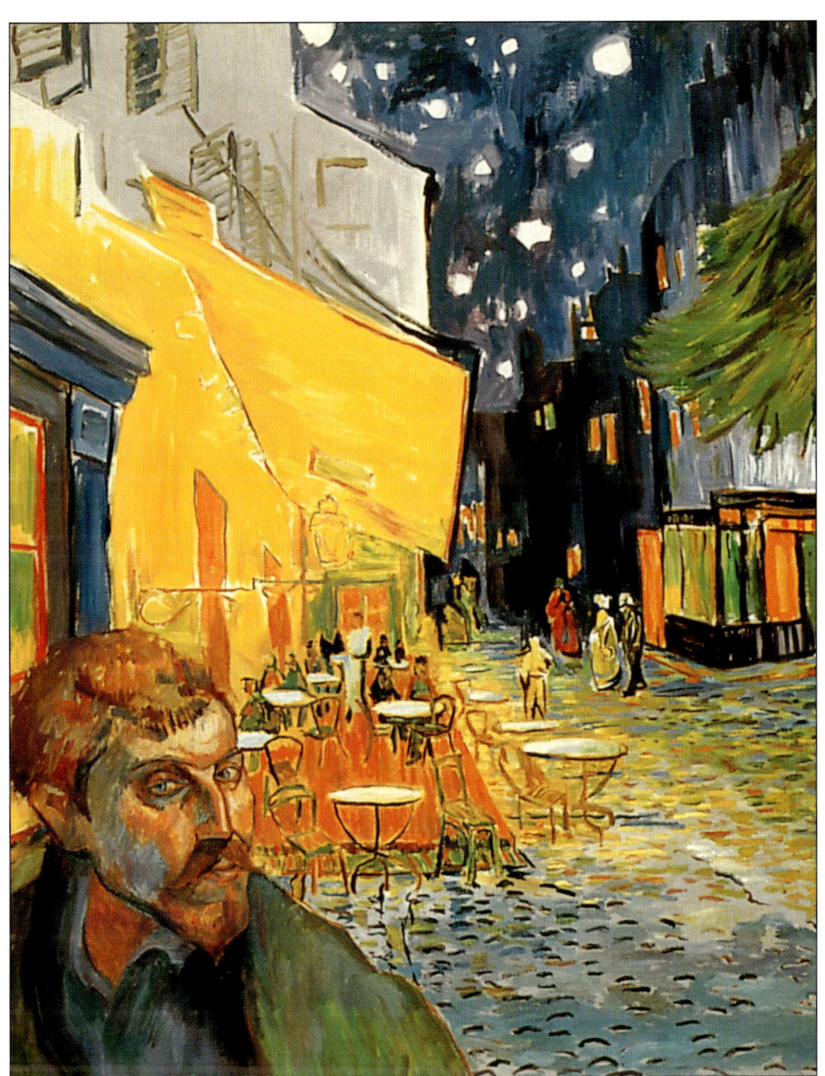

I Don't Know, Vincent, What Do *You* Want to Do Tonight?

1993, 40 x 30 inches

Source

Van Gogh, *Self-Portrait,* 1890, Musée d'Orsay, Paris

"You're a slow learner, ja, Connor?" said Josef Albers, my teacher at Yale. When I looked at the painting years later and realized what was so obviously missing, I looked for the late self-portrait that summed up Vincent for me. Then I changed the direction of Gauguin's gaze so that he addresses the question directly to his friend.

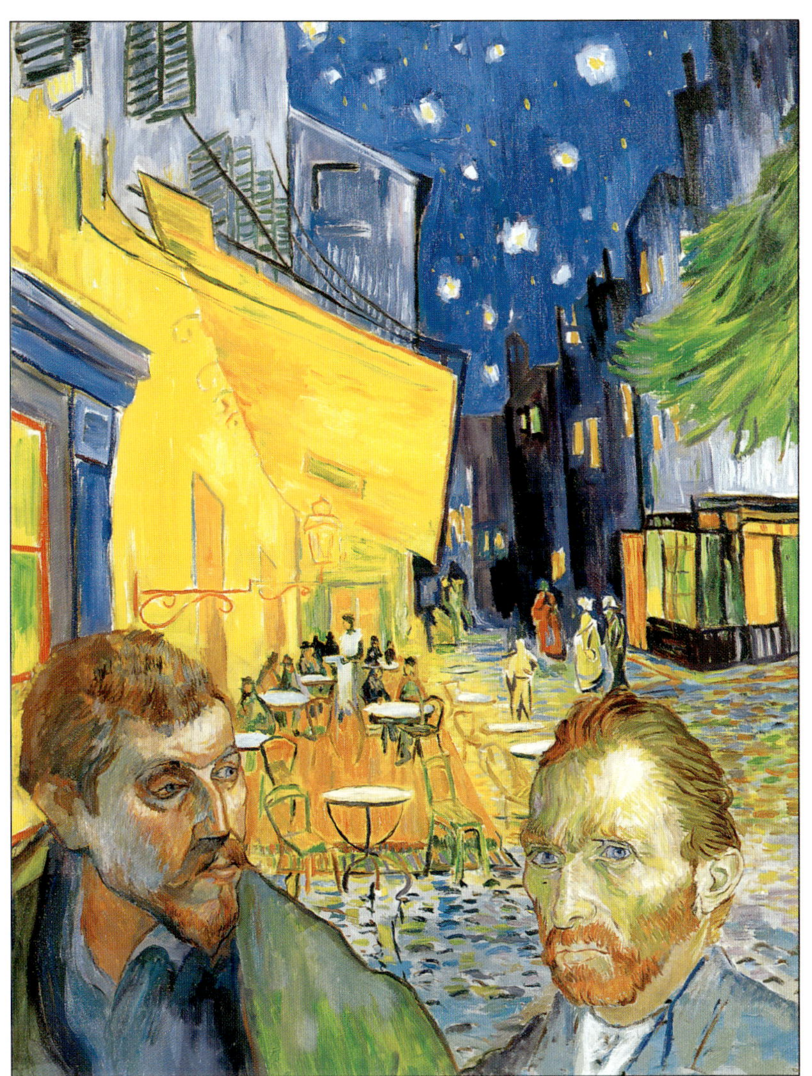

The Pundits and the Whatsit

1992, 40 x 30 inches

Sources

Rembrandt, *The Anatomy Lesson of Dr. Tulp* (detail), 1632, Hague Municipal Museum, The Hague

Warhol, *Brillo Box,* 1964, private collection, New York

Among his many virtues, the philosopher-critic Arthur Danto is the most courteous of men. If he had any doubts when I responded to his inquiry about whether I had an appropriate painting to propose for the cover of his new book by saying, "Let me look around," he did not voice them. Sure enough, when he came to the studio a few days later, I had miraculously unearthed this painting, which seemed to fit the bill perfectly. His book, a collection of essays in art criticism, is called *Beyond the Brillo Box*. The title refers to the Warhol art objects that, when they made their startling appearance in Leo Castelli's gallery in 1964, appeared to him to bring conventional art history to a close and move it into the realm of philosophy. I am less enthusiastic than Arthur about the direction of art since that event, but I suspect that, like the influence of television, that day in 1964 helped to make these paintings possible.

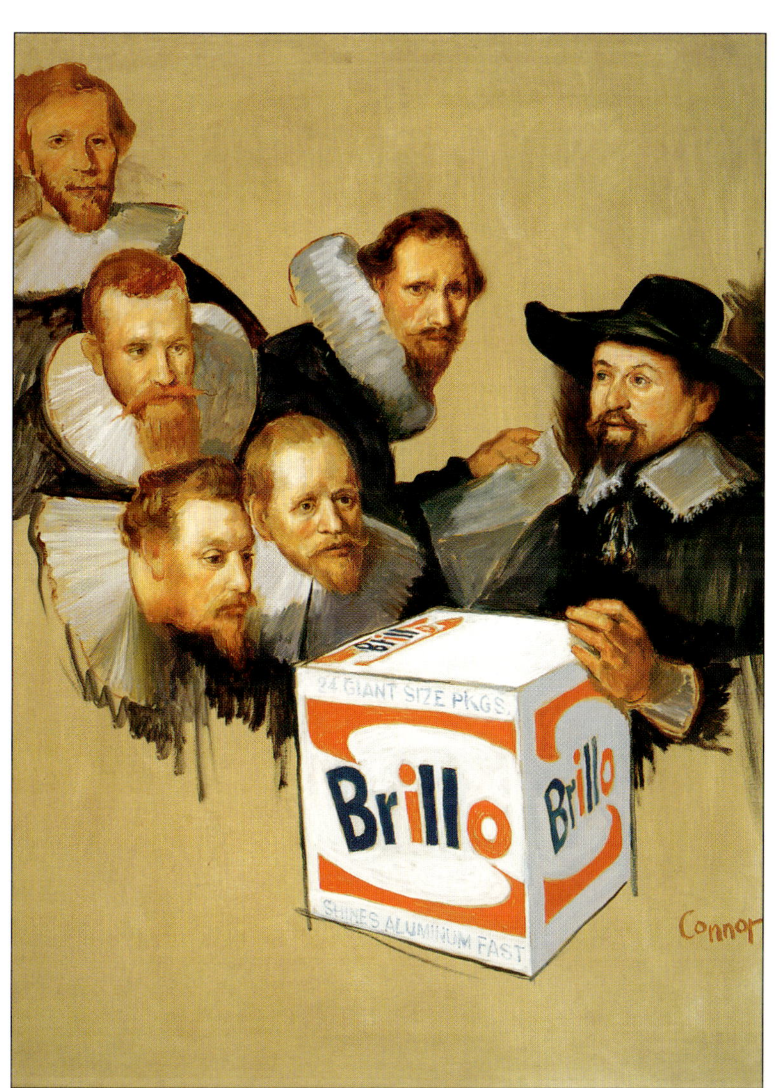
24 GIANT SIZE PKGS.
Brillo
Brillo
SHINES ALUMINUM FAST
Connor

Not Myself Today

1992, 40 x 30 inches

Sources

Picasso, *Girl with Mirror,* 1932, Museum of Modern Art, New York

Sargent, *Madame X* (Madame Pierre Gautreau), 1884, Metropolitan Museum of Art, New York

One of the innovations that Tina Brown brought as editor to *The New Yorker* in 1992 was the notion that the subject of the cover should as often as possible relate to the content of the magazine. The art director, who knew my work, told me that an upcoming issue would prominently feature an essay about fashion and asked if I had any paintings that might relate to that topic. *The New Yorker* had played such a major role in the after-school side of my formation that I was determined not to miss the chance to be a part of it. I had always wanted to do something with Picasso's *Girl with Mirror.* Searching through art books, I auditioned a few women for the role of her startling mirror image before deciding on Sargent's notorious *Madame X.* When I reversed her direction, the two great profiles finally faced off. Feeling very up-to-date, I faxed a sketch of it to the magazine and got the OK. It appeared on the November 23, 1992, cover. It may have more to do with vanity and narcissism than fashion, except perhaps the fashions of the world of art.

After seeing the painting printed with *The New Yorker's* logo on top, I thought it looked odd without it, so I lettered it back in.

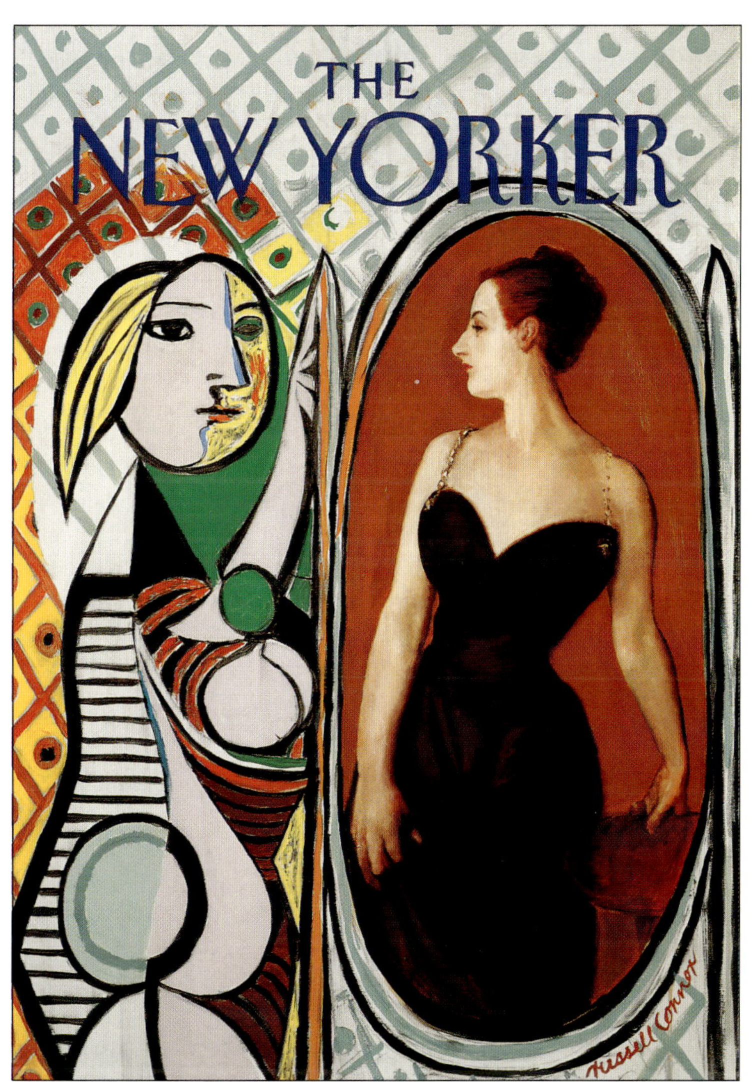
THE
NEW YORKER
Russell Connor

Between Art and Life

1996, 48 x 48 inches

Sources

Manet, *Luncheon on the Grass,* 1863, Musée d'Orsay, Paris

Manet, *Self-Portrait with Palette,* 1878, private collection, New York

Fantin-Latour, *Portrait of Edouard Manet,* 1867, Art Institute of Chicago

It seems fitting to conclude with Manet, who has been my favorite silent partner in this reckless and rewarding adventure. There actually exists a drawing that shows him painting in his top hat and frock coat. This image of him is a composite, in which I took the Rembrandtesque portrait of him by his friend Fantin-Latour, turned him a little toward us, and replaced the cane in his hands with the brushes and palette from a later self-portrait. It began as a commission for a cover of *The New York Times Book Review* that featured a laudatory notice by James Mellow of a new biography entitled *Manet: Rebel in a Frock Coat* by Beth Archer Brombert. Leaving space for text, I placed him in a rather abstract, bare studio, where two models (Victorine Meurent and his soon-to-be brother-in-law, Ferdinand Leenhoff) are posing for his first scandalous masterpiece, *Luncheon on the Grass*.

After its appearance in the *Times*, the life of this work as an illustration was over, and I completed it as a painting, adding a sketchy copy of his lovely still life of picnic basket and abandoned clothing.

Salut, dear Manet. *Salut* to all the great ones who have been such marvelous company, and *salut* to the reader, who perhaps smiled and then saw something beyond the joke, for making the adventure complete.

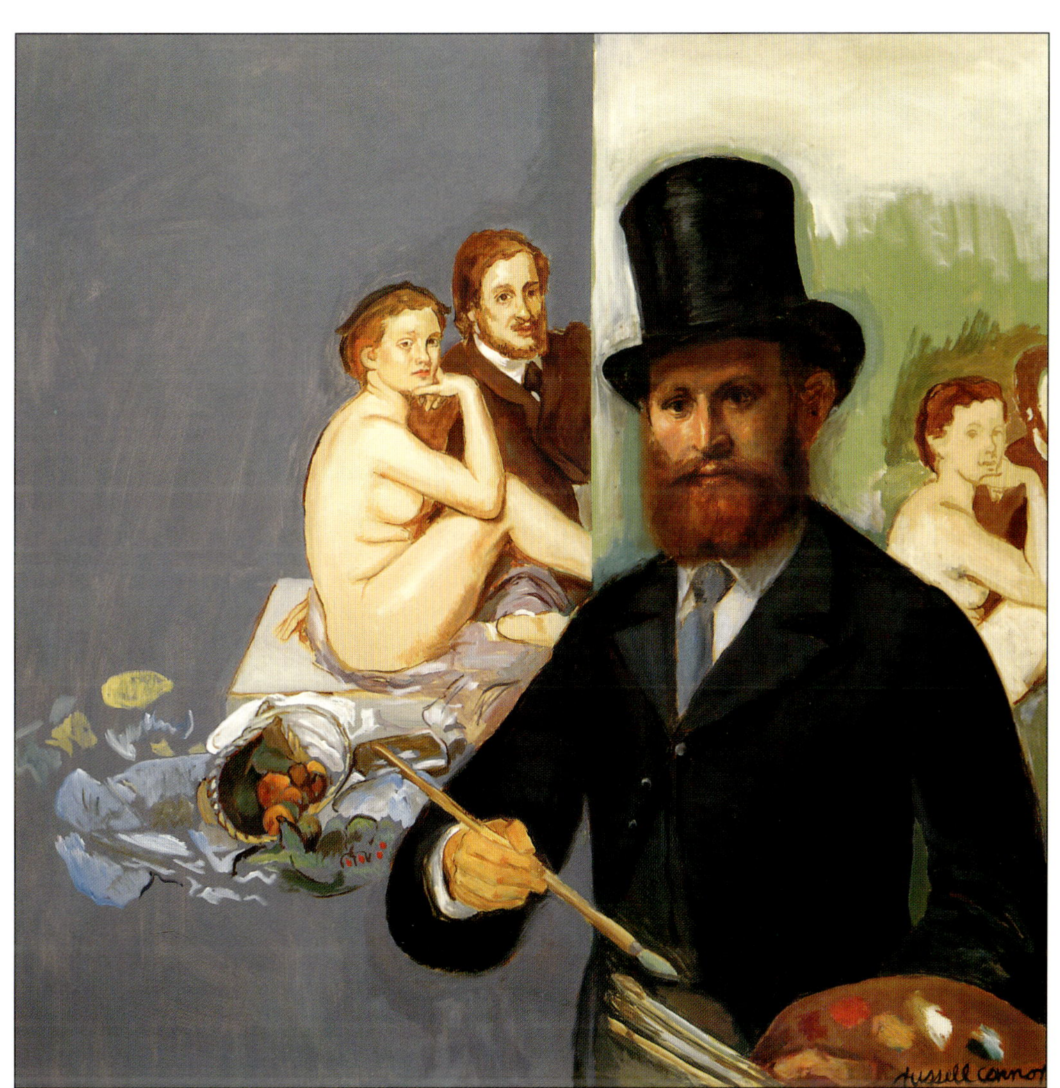
Russell Connor

List of Plates